W9-BWF-452

507
G
c·1 Gardner, Robert
Science in your back-
yard

34 8860000082/848

DATE DUE

507
Gar
c.1

34 88 0000 82 848

BOOK CHARGING CARD

Accession No. _____ Call No. _____

Author _Gardner, Robert_

Title _Science in your back-_
yard

Date Loaned	Borrower's Name	Date Returned

SCIENCE
IN YOUR
BACKYARD

SCIENCE
IN YOUR
BACKYARD

ROBERT GARDNER
DAVID WEBSTER

ILLUSTRATED WITH PHOTOGRAPHS
AND LINE DRAWINGS

Julian Messner 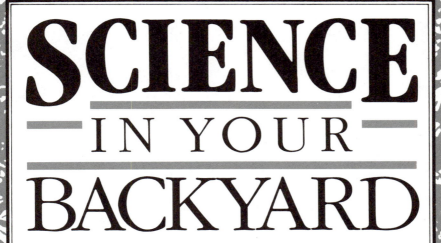 New York
A Division of Simon & Schuster, Inc.

507
G
c-1

Cover photo: Robert Frerck, 1984/Woodfin Camp & Associates

JULIAN MESSNER and colophon are trademarks
of Simon & Schuster, Inc.

10 9 8 7 6 5 4 3 2 1 (lib. ed.)
10 9 8 7 6 5 4 3 2 1 (pbk. ed.)

Manufactured in the United States of America

Library of Congress Cataloguing in Publication Data

Webster, David, 1930–
Science in your backyard.

1. Science—Experiments. 2. Scientific reactions.
I. Gardner, Robert, 1929–   . II. Title.
Q164.W424 1987 507′.8 86-21817
ISBN: 0-671-55565-0 (lib. ed.)
0-671-63835-1 (pbk. ed.)

CONTENTS

PREFACE

Many people think that scientists spend all their time in a laboratory, but that is not true. Scientists have conducted experiments and made observations in many different places, from beneath the ocean's surface to the far side of the moon.

Your backyard, rooftop, park, or playground is a good place to carry out a number of interesting investigations. There you can find a great variety of insects and other small animals. Some are difficult to see, but you can find them by looking closely at soil, trees, leaves, and puddles, under rocks and bark, even in the air. It's also a good place to set up a weather station, observe and map the movements of the sun, moon, and various constellations, construct your own pond or tidal pool, plant seeds, and grow your own vegetable or weed garden. You can study the shadows that cross your yard, and observe the larger plants and animals that live there, as well as the signs that indicate the presence of nocturnal animals that you may never see.

These are a few of the scientific observations and experiments that this book will help you carry out in your own backyard, rooftop, park, or playground. In addition, we'll guide you on trips beyond your yard to visit a pond, an ocean, and places where you can collect rocks. So let's go outside and do some science. We think you'll enjoy it.

SCIENCE
IN YOUR
BACKYARD

1

INSECT SAFARI

Insects make good pets. They are easy to catch and can be kept alive in simple cages. You can assemble a collection of dead insects by mounting them on pins in a display box.

Insects are everywhere. They fly through the air, dig under the soil, and swim in the water. Insects live in leaves, underneath bark, in fruits, and even inside your home. Warm days in the summer and early fall are the best times to look for bugs.

GO ON AN INSECT HUNT

Before starting your insect search, you should get suitable containers for carrying them home. Small plastic vials are probably the best things to use. Drugstores have vials that are used for dispensing pills. It is not necessary to make holes in the caps since insects breath very little air.

You might look first in the grass on your lawn or at a playground. Get down on your knees and

paw through the blades of grass with your hands. Sometimes it is a good idea just to sit still and watch for something moving. You should be able to find beetles, ants, leaf hoppers, grasshoppers, and crickets. There are some insects you should be careful of, like bees and wasps. Also be careful of spiders and ticks, which are arachnids.

Other insects live in tall plants such as weeds, garden flowers, and vegetables. Look inside flowers and underneath leaves. Some insects eat just one type of plant. The milkweed beetle, for example, is usually found only on milkweed plants. The tomato hornworm got its name because it feeds on tomato leaves.

The best time to look for moths and other nocturnal insects is at night. They are attracted by light, so check outside your windows and near street lights after dark.

You might attract insects by putting some food outdoors. Fruit flies, bees, and wasps often congregate around pieces of apple, banana, and other fruit. Rotten meat attracts other kinds of flies looking for places to deposit eggs.

An easy way to find insects that live in bushes and trees is to shake them onto the ground. Place a white sheet or large piece of plastic under the branches before you start. Then shake the branches as hard as you can or beat them with a big stick. You will be surprised by how many insects fall on the sheet.

CATCHING INSECTS WITH A SWEEP NET

Flying insects are almost impossible to catch without a good net. Butterfly nets are sold by the

How to Make a Sweep Net

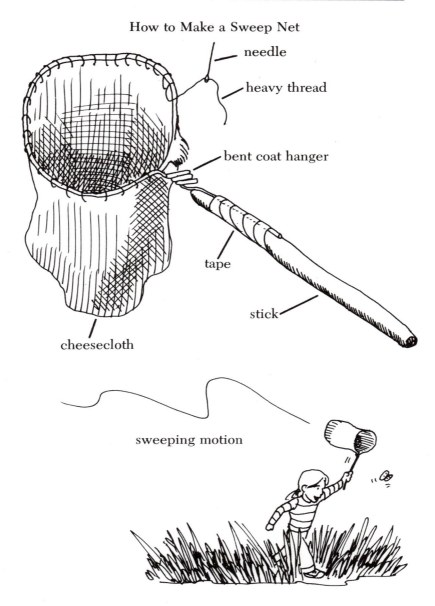

needle

heavy thread

bent coat hanger

tape

stick

cheesecloth

sweeping motion

science supply companies listed in the Appendix. You can make your own sweep net by sewing a piece of cheesecloth or flexible netting to a wire loop, like a bent coat hanger. Fasten the handle of the loop securely to a strong pole, using lots of twine or plastic electrical tape. Use the net to catch such flying insects as butterflies, moths, dragonflies, and mosquitoes.

You can catch insects hiding in weeds and long grass by sweeping your net back and forth in a figure-8 motion. Keep the net moving so any trapped insects cannot escape by flying out. When you want to stop and check your catch, flop the lower part of the net over the loop. Keep the net away from bushes and thorns so it does not get ripped.

FINDING SOIL INSECTS

Insects that live in the soil often can be found hiding under rocks or rotten leaves. You could also dig up the soil with a trowel or small shovel. Place the dirt on a cloth and go through it carefully with your hands.

Some beetles and ants live in rotten wood. Look for a dead tree that is still standing or has fallen to the ground. Pull off the bark to find insects hiding underneath. When you find a rotten piece of wood on the ground, break it apart with your hands or a hammer. Work on a piece of white cloth so the ants, beetles, earwigs, or other insects cannot crawl away before you see them.

CATCHING WATER INSECTS

You probably do not have a pond in your backyard, but there may be one nearby. Swamps and shallow ponds with waterweeds usually have more insects than do rocky lakes and streams.

Sometimes land and air insects fall into the water and drown. Look for bodies of dead bugs floating on the surface.

You can catch live water insects in a jar or plastic food container. Water striders scoot along on the surface, and mosquito larvae and diving beetles swim underneath.

Insects hiding on the bottom can be caught with a kitchen strainer. Bend back the two "ears" on the front of the strainer so you can scoop through the rotting vegetation on the bottom of the pond. Dump out the contents of the strainer and sort through the mud with your fingers. You might find some nymphs, which are the immature stages of dragonflies, caddisflies, and other flying insects.

INSECT TRAPS

Insects can be caught in traps that you can make. Of course, an insect trap is different from a mouse trap or a bear trap.

A tin can is all you need to trap insects that crawl on top of the ground. Find a secluded spot in your garden or under a bush in a city park. Dig a hole for the can so its top is level with the ground. It is a good idea to put a little water in the bottom of the trap so the insects that fall in might drown before they have a chance to crawl out. Also, you can use bait to lure insects into the can. Make a mixture from two parts molasses and one part water.

Since many insects are attracted to light, you can make a trap for nocturnal insects with a light

A Simple Light Trap

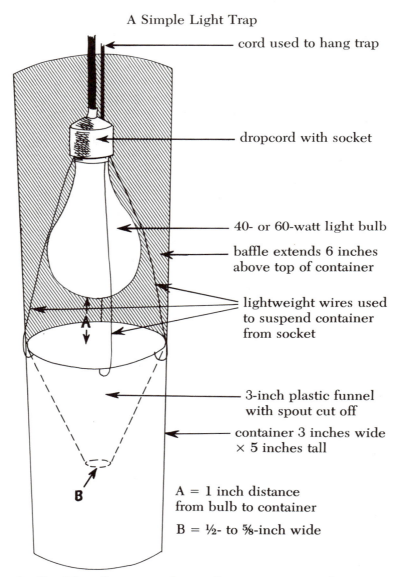

cord used to hang trap

dropcord with socket

40- or 60-watt light bulb

baffle extends 6 inches
above top of container

lightweight wires used
to suspend container
from socket

3-inch plastic funnel
with spout cut off

container 3 inches wide
× 5 inches tall

A = 1 inch distance
from bulb to container

B = ½- to ⅝-inch wide

bulb. The drawing shows how to suspend a container and funnel under the bulb. At night, insects fly into the light, fall into the trap, and are
unable to escape.

LUCKY FINDS

Often you discover a good insect when you are not on a bug hunt. You just happen to spot a big bee inside your car or a colorful beetle strolling along the sidewalk. To be ready for such moments, carry a vial in your pocket at all times.

YOUR INSECT ZOO

It is not hard to make a cage for keeping live insects. The simplest is just a wide-mouthed glass jar covered on top with a piece of fine netting or cloth. Keep the netting in place with a rubber

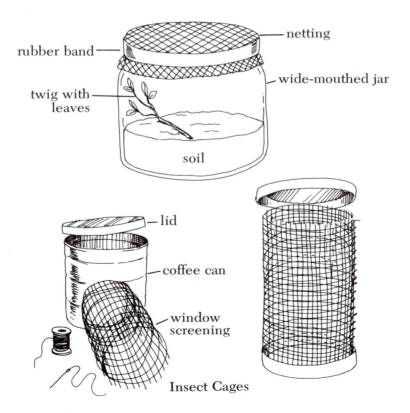

Insect Cages

band. Place a thin layer of damp soil and decaying leaves in the bottom of the jar to provide the insects with moisture and protection.

You can make a bigger cage from a coffee can and a piece of window screening. Roll the screen into a cylinder so that one end fits into the can. You may sew the screen together with heavy thread if you wish. Add loose soil and leaf litter for moisture. Cover the open end of the screening with the can's lid or a second can.

A terrarium in a glass aquarium is another suitable habitat for captive air and land insects. Water insects, of course, would have to be kept separately in an aquarium filled with pond water.

In order to stay alive, insects need air, water, food, and the proper temperature. Add drops of water to the insect cage when the materials on the bottom start to dry out. If you find an insect on a leaf, feed it fresh leaves from the same kind of plant. Some insects may eat dead insects. Keep the insect cage out of the sun.

DEAD INSECTS

There are special places to look for dead insects. Insects that fly into your house by mistake try to get out through the windows because they are attracted by the outside light. There almost always are dead bugs on any windowsill between the inside window and the outside storm window.

Insects are also attracted to the ceiling lights in your house. When they die, the bugs fall into the glass covers under the light bulbs. Have an adult help you take down the covers so you can collect the bodies inside.

Many insects are killed when they are hit by moving cars. The insects are blown through the car's grill and get stuck on the front of the radiator. Lift the hood of a car or truck so you can collect traffic victims inside. Be sure to get permission from the driver of the car, however, and be sure the engine is not running or hot.

MOUNTED INSECT COLLECTION

The photograph following shows part of an insect collection made by a boy in Massachusetts. When an insect is caught alive, it is killed by chemicals in a killing jar. Pins are used to mount the insects neatly in the box. When identified, each insect can be labeled.

To make a killing jar, you need a small glass jar with a screw cap. Put ten to twenty drops of rubbing alcohol into the jar, place the insects inside, close the jar, and keep the cap in place. The alcohol fumes should kill bugs in several hours.

Special pins are made for pinning insects; they are sold by the science supply companies listed in the Appendix. The pins come in different sizes; for your work, #2 and #3 would be best. You can use ordinary straight pins or map pins as a substitute, but they are thicker and shorter than the black pins made for insect collections.

If an insect has a large body, push the pin carefully through its back. If the insect is small, glue it first to the top of a slender paper triangle. Then insert the pin through the base of the paper. La-

An insect collection made by a boy in Massachusetts. The insects are labeled and mounted on Styrofoam.

carolina grashopper

fall webworm

bel each insect with its name, the date, and the place where you captured it.

Remember to handle the insect gently so that its legs, wings, or antennae do not break. A pair of fine tweezers, known as forceps, will help. You can use a magnifying glass to study the structure of your insects.

The box to house your insect collection should be made of wood or heavy cardboard. It should be 2 to 3 inches deep and have a cover. Cut a piece of corrugated cardboard or thin Styrofoam to fit into the bottom of the box. Over this glue a piece of white paper. You can purchase a sturdier box from a science supply company.

Arrange the insects in neat rows. As your collection grows, you may need to use additional boxes.

You should put a mothball or some moth crystals into one corner of the box to kill tiny museum beetles that often invade insect collections and eat them.

INSECT LIFE CYCLES

One of the most interesting things about insects is their varied life cycles. All insects begin as *eggs*. The eggs of most insects hatch into the *larva* stage. The larva of a butterfly or a moth is called a caterpillar, a mosquito larva is called a wriggler, and a fly larva is a maggot or grub. After the larva has grown, it changes into the *pupa* stage. Dramatic transformations occur within the pupa until the *adult* insect emerges. Some insects, such as crickets and praying mantises, have eggs that hatch directly into miniature adult forms.

The eggs of most insects are too small to find. The praying mantis, though, lays her eggs in a frothy mass that hardens into a blob resembling a piece of brown sponge. Look for these on the stems of goldenrod and other tall plants in the fall.

Caterpillars are often found feeding on the leaves of plants and trees. Sometimes the presence of caterpillars can be detected by plant leaves that have been chewed. Some caterpillars, such as the tent caterpillar in the spring and the fall webworm in late summer, live in messy webbed shelters. If you find one, cut it out intact, place it in a cage, and watch it.

When you catch a caterpillar, remember to collect a supply of leaves from the plant it was eating. House the caterpillar in a jar along with some leaves for food. If you are lucky, the caterpillar will continue to eat and then turn into a cocoon inside the jar. The pupal stage of a butterfly is called a chrysalid; only moths make cocoons.

Cocoons and chrysalids can be found in the fall. Search the cracks in the corners of your house and in rough tree bark. After the leaves have fallen, look for cocoons attached to stands of dead weed stalks.

If you want to see a cocoon or chrysalid hatch, you must keep it cold for several months to simulate winter conditions. You could store the cocoon in your refrigerator or outside for part of the winter. When you return the cocoon to the warmth of your home, it might hatch in several weeks.

Sometimes insect larvae or pupae can be found inside a *gall*. Galls are abnormal growths on leaves caused by insects. The developing larvae inside the gall are protected from many enemies and have a built-in food supply.

Look for bumps and swellings on oak leaves and plant stems. You can cut open galls with a knife to study the hidden occupants inside. You may keep other galls intact and watch them to see if mature insects emerge later.

INSECT IDENTIFICATION

It is hard to identify insects because there are so many different kinds. A good reference book from your school or local library is essential.

Insects are grouped into different families known as *orders*. As your insect collection grows, you might want to group the insects by families in separate boxes.

On the next page is a sample list of selected insect families.

All insects are characterized by six legs and two antennae. They have three body parts: a head, a thorax, and an abdomen.

In searching for insects, you will find creatures that might look like insects, but are not. Spiders and daddy longlegs have eight legs and are *arachnids*. Centipedes, millipedes, and sowbugs are often found hiding under rocks.

You could display all noninsects in a separate collection box.

ORDER	EXAMPLES
Orthoptera	Cockroaches
	Grasshoppers
	Crickets
Odonata	Dragonflies
	Damselflies
Hemiptera	Stink bugs
	Water striders
	Leaf hoppers
Coleoptera	Beetles
	Weevils
Hymenoptera	Bees
	Wasps
	Ants
Lepidoptera	Butterflies
	Moths
Diptera	Flies
	Mosquitoes

2

SIGNS OF WILD ANIMALS

What animals live in your yard, at the playground, or in the park? You may have seen squirrels or an occasional rabbit. Yet there probably are many other animals that you have never seen, shy animals that come out at night. All animals leave behind signs of their activities. By reading these telltale records, you can learn about the secret lives of animals that live in your neighborhood.

FINDING TRACKS

Animals leave tracks only when they walk across snow or soft ground. After a rain, look for tracks in muddy places in a garden, along dirt paths, and next to roads where cars wear out the grass. The best time of year to find tracks in mud is during the spring as the ground thaws out.

Animals always leave tracks in snow, but those in deep snow usually are unclear. The best condition for seeing tracks is a thin covering of snow, especially if it is wet.

Instead of waiting for mud or snow, you can make powder "traps" to record animal footprints. Sprinkle any powdery substance, such as flour, pancake mix, or baking soda in a circle about three feet across. Spread the powder only in dry places, since damp powder gets sticky and hard. Place some bait in the center of the circle each evening.

Sometimes cats leave tracks when they walk on the dusty hood of a dirty car.

PRESERVING TRACKS

To aid in future identification, you should keep a record of the size and shape of each track. The quickest way is to make a drawing. Put in all the details you can and include measurements made with a ruler.

If you have a camera, you could take photographs of tracks. Take pictures in the early morning or late in the day so that the low sun highlights the track impression. Include a ruler in the photo to show scale.

To cast tracks made in soft ground with plaster of Paris, first ring the track with a collar made from heavy paper. Mix the plaster with water to the consistency of melted ice cream. If the plaster is too thick, it might not fill in the narrower parts of the track. Watery plaster, on the other hand, takes longer to harden and may become powdery when dry. Pour the soupy plaster into the collar and allow it to harden for several hours.

Tracks in snow cannot be preserved too well with plaster. Use hot paraffin instead. This liquid wax hardens instantly when it comes into contact with the freezing snow. You can buy blocks of

How to Cast Plaster Tracks

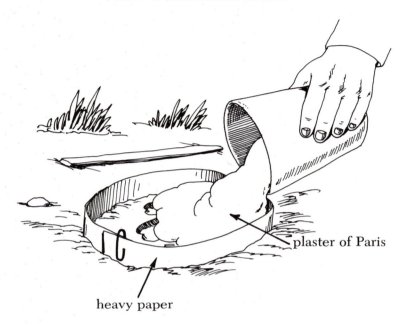

plaster of Paris

heavy paper

paraffin in the supermarket. Ask an adult to help you melt the paraffin or some candles in an old pan on the kitchen stove. Be careful not to touch the paraffin when it is heated. As you pour the heated wax into the snow track, try to cover it first with just a thin layer. Build up the thickness of the wax a little at a time by allowing each layer to cool for a few seconds.

IDENTIFYING TRACKS

Probably most of the tracks you find will have been made by dogs or cats. Cat tracks are smaller and never show nail marks. The four feet of a dog or cat are almost always the same size. A hopping animal, such as a rabbit or squirrel, has hind feet

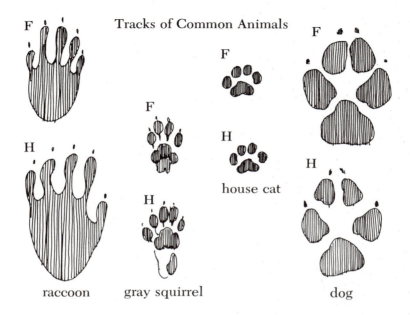

Tracks of Common Animals

house cat

raccoon   gray squirrel   dog

much larger than the front feet. Since skunks and porcupines walk flat-footed, their tracks are relatively large.

Your school or local library should have reference books to help you identify the tracks you find.

REMAINS OF FOOD

Animals spend most of their lives either sleeping or searching for food. The presence of unseen animals is often revealed by their feeding litter.

Squirrels leave piles of cracked acorns and beechnuts below places where they sit to eat. They discard the nutshells after devouring the softer parts inside. The great power of a squirrel's incisor teeth is shown by its ability to gnaw through the tough shells of black walnuts and hickory nuts. Red squirrels relish the seeds from pinecones. They rip off the scales of the pine-cones, leaving piles of scales and bare center stems.

A mouse eats nuts without breaking them apart. Its pointed snout allows it to feast on the nut meat through a small hole gnawed into the end.

Other gnawing animals such as rabbits, meadow mice, and porcupines feed on the tender bark of tree trunks and branches. Cottontail rabbits prefer the bark of sumac and fruit trees. The light wood of skinned branches is especially noticeable during the winter, when other plant foods are scarce.

Gnawed bones are usually a sign of dogs. Even after all the meat has been removed, a dog will continue to chew the bone in an attempt to reach the flavorful marrow inside. Porcupines gnaw on bones, too, but they seek the minerals of the bone itself.

A scattering of feathers usually marks a cat-and-bird encounter. The cat's needlelike toenails and teeth are designed for catching and eating small animals.

Skunks are fond of grubs and other insects that live in the soil. The skunk paws at the soil with a front foot, moving it in a circular motion. You may have seen small skunk holes dug in your lawn or in pine needles and leaves under trees.

Woodpeckers, too, leave signs of food-foraging efforts. With their long beaks, they hammer into bark and rotting wood, probing for tasty insects. The sapsucker makes lines of regularly spaced holes in the soft bark of apple and aspen trees. The woodpecker returns to the holes later to find insects that have become trapped in the sap ooz-ing from the holes.

ANIMAL HOMES

Some animals build homes for protection, for raising their young, and for storing food. Small animals need a shelter to protect them from their many enemies. Most larger animals are strong enough to survive without any kind of home.

A woodchuck often digs its burrow in an open field. The den has two openings: the main en-trance where the soil is pushed out, and the smaller back door. Its sleeping quarters at the bottom might be four or five feet below the sur-face. Other small animals that live in dens are skunks, badgers, foxes, and prairie dogs.

Moles rarely emerge from their underground tunnels. When close to the surface, moles dig by pushing the soil upward to form the long ridges you may have seen in a lawn or garden. They make deeper tunnels in a different fashion, dig-ging a short distance into the soil, then turning around and pushing the loose earth to the surface to form a molehill.

A chipmunk's burrow is hard to notice because there is no loose soil around the single entrance. The secret to the chipmunk's inconspicuous door is its clever excavation technique. It digs a tun-nel with two entrances about three feet apart. Then it piles all the excavated soil around one opening, sealing it off.

Many varieties of mice nest in underground burrows. The field mouse uses a burrow in the winter, but spends its summer vacation in a hollowed-out cavity between clumps of grass. White-footed mice make their homes in a variety of places. Some live in burrows, while others build nests in hollow logs, knotholes, or abandoned bird nests.

SQUIRREL NESTS

Look in treetops for gray squirrel nests made with leaves and sticks. The nests are best spotted during the winter months after the leaves have fallen. The foundation of the gray squirrel nest is made in the crotch of a tree from rather stout sticks and branches. The large leaves covering the top make the nest fairly waterproof. The inside of the nest is lined with soft grass or moss. Some large birds also make leaf nests, but these are not rounded on top as are squirrel nests.

During the winter, gray squirrels usually move to a hollow tree. A snug nest of dead leaves is used as a nursery for the baby squirrels, which are born in the early spring.

Red squirrels and flying squirrels also make their homes in hollow trees, knotholes, and woodpecker holes.

BIRD NESTS

You probably can find bird nests by looking carefully in the branches of bushes and trees. Nests are easier to find after the leaves have fallen. Keep low and look up so any nest is silhouetted against the bright sky.

It is all right to collect nests except in the springtime, when the birds are raising their families.

Nests are fragile and must be protected if handled. The nest materials can be held together by varnish. You can apply it from a spray can or dip the nest in a small bowl of varnish. When the nest is dry, glue it to a stiff piece of cardboard and label it.

It is not easy to identify nests. Nest size is an obvious clue; small birds make smaller nests than large birds. The location of the nest is also important. Redwing blackbirds nest in swamp reeds, while the Baltimore oriole's nest hangs from the tip of a high tree branch.

Birds use all kinds of materials for nest making. Robin and grackle nests are distinctive because of the hard shell fashioned from grass and mud. The catbird weaves its loose nest with grape bark, while a goldfinch uses thistledown. Other birds use twigs, roots, birch bark, moss, horsehair, or string. You could help birds in the spring by providing them with a supply of short pieces of colored yarn and other nest-building materials.

For the identification of the nests in your collection, you will need a good reference book. It will provide identifications based on the size of the nest, the materials used in its construction, and the location where you found the nest.

Bird eggs sometimes fall out of a nest before hatching. The blue-green color of robins' eggs makes them easy to recognize. White eggshells of pigeons can be found in city streets.

FEATHER COLLECTION

Feathers occasionally fall off birds as they fly or move about on the ground. If you look for feathers, you might not be able to find any right away. Feathers usually are found by chance. Whenever you spot one, save it for later examination.

You might be able to pick up special kinds of feathers at a zoo aviary, at pet shops that sell parrots or finches, or at a poultry farm.

Perhaps you can figure out from what bird each feather came. Color is one of a feather's most distinguishing characteristics. A blue feather could be from a blue jay, while a white one might be a pigeon's.

Size is important, too, although any one bird has feathers of quite different sizes. Larger feathers on the wings, body, and tail are known as *contour* feathers. Contour feathers are used in making arrows and as decorations on hats. American Indians displayed large feathers as symbols of their religion, loyalty to a tribe, and a warrior's courage. Quill pens for writing with ink were once made by shaping the quill of a contour feather with a penknife.

The smaller, fuzzy feathers are called *down* feathers. These provide the bird with a layer of effective insulation when the weather is cold. Perhaps you have down feathers inside a pillow, a winter jacket, or a sleeping bag.

Compare the structure of a feather you find with the one shown in the drawing. If you have a microscope, clip off some barbs and look at them with it. Can you see how the barbules hold the barbs stiff to make a strong but lightweight sur-

Parts of a Feather

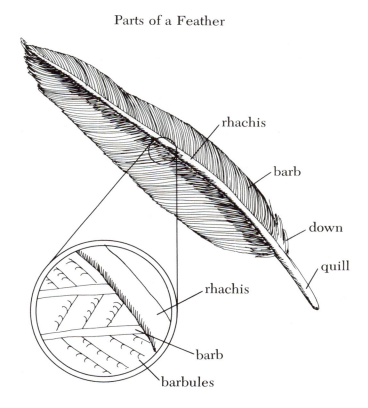

face? Velcro fasteners were invented by someone who knew how feather barbules stick together.

BONES AND FUR

Animal bones are found quite frequently because they take such a long time to rot away. As soon as an animal dies, its body is attacked by other animals that feed on dead meat. Dogs, coyotes, cats, and crows relish the flesh they can tear from carcasses. Any fragments of meat remaining on the chewed bones are devoured quickly by ants, beetles, maggots, and other insects. Ultimately, after a final cleaning by bacteria, bones become bleached white by the sun.

Most of the bones found outside are left by dogs. Dogs often bury bones and do not often dig them up later. Such bones last underground for twenty years or more.

Sometimes the skeleton of an animal remains somewhat intact on top of the ground. Missing parts can be attributed to damage from scavengers. Bird bodies decay more quickly because of their small size.

An owl eats small birds and rodents by swallowing them whole. Later, the owl regurgitates the indigestible parts in a dry pellet. If you find a wad of hair and bones, pull it apart and glue the tiny bones to a card for identification.

You will have to be a real detective to identify bones. Long bones usually come from the legs, while a rounder bone with a hole in the center is a vertebra from the backbone.

The skull provides the easiest identification. Consider its size. It is always somewhat smaller than the animal's head, because a live creature's skull is covered with flesh and hair.

Teeth are an important clue to the animal's diet. *Rodents,* such as squirrels and woodchucks, have four large incisors in front for gnawing plants and bark. Other *herbivores,* or plant eaters, have smaller incisors for clipping off grass and leaves, but large molars in the back of the mouth for chewing. Animals that eat meat are called *carnivores.* The large canine teeth of cats, dogs, foxes, and raccoons are used for killing and for tearing flesh.

Many of the bones you find may have originated in the supermarket. They are bones from people's kitchens: the remains of steaks, roasts, and chops. You can usually recognize a supermarket bone by one or more flat surfaces made by the butcher's hacksaw.

Be on the lookout, too, for wads of fur stuck on thorns or broken twigs. Rabbits, squirrels, and other animals occasionally lose fur when scurrying through low bushes.

DEAD ANIMALS

Where do you see dead animals? If you drive through the country, you certainly have noticed animals that were killed along the road. Perhaps you have seen bodies of porcupines, squirrels, skunks, raccoons, opossums, woodchucks, or even deer.

It is unusual to find a dead animal in your backyard because the carcass is consumed so quickly by hungry scavengers.

What can cause an animal's death? Some animals are killed by cats or dogs. Occasionally animals have accidents just like people. Birds crash into windows, and squirrels fall from trees. Other animals die of disease, starvation, or old age.

LIVE ANIMALS

Diurnal animals are active in the daytime, and these are the ones you have the best chance to see. Squirrels, rabbits, chipmunks, woodchucks,

An Animal Trap

1. Use a sturdy box with a lid attached.

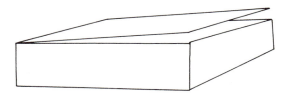

2. Whittle three sticks of wood, as shown in the side and top views.

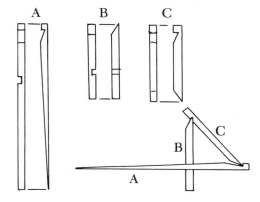

3. Put a piece of food on the pointed end of the long stick, and set up the trap.

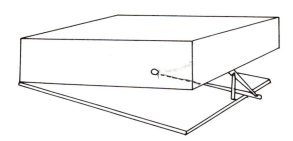

and most birds are diurnal. You can attract birds to your yard with feeders and bird houses. If you do spot an animal, spend a little time observing its behavior.

Watch squirrels jumping in the treetops. How does the squirrel use its tail to help it maintain balance? How far can it jump? What does the squirrel do if you get too close? How does a squirrel react when another squirrel approaches? Are there ways you can tell one squirrel from another?

Other animals are *nocturnal*, or active at night. Raccoons, skunks, opossums, foxes, and owls sleep during the day and hunt for food after dark, when it is safer. You can look around outside at night with a flashlight in search of nocturnal animals. Move slowly and quietly. Place some bait— a meat bone, bread, or vegetables—in an open spot that you can watch from inside your home.

TRAPPING

Traps for catching live animals can be bought in many hardware stores. The traps are manufactured by the Hav-a-Hart Company and come in different sizes. If an animal ventures into the trap to take the bait, the doors fall down and lock closed.

The drawings opposite and on the next page show two traps you can make yourself. The box of the figure-4 trap drops on a larger animal when it touches the bait. You can catch smaller animals in the one made from a tin can and mouse trap.

If you are successful in trapping a wild animal,

watch it for a while and then release it. Do not handle the animal. It is not a good idea to keep a trapped animal for a pet. Never keep raccoons or foxes, since their bite could give you rabies. Try to release the animal in the same area where you caught it.

Tin Can Trap

1. Tape an ice pop stick to the trigger of a mouse trap.

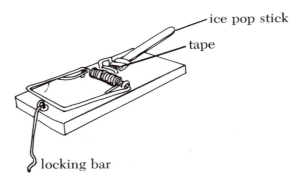

ice pop stick

tape

locking bar

2. With a hammer and nail make four holes in a large coffee or juice can.

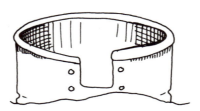

3. Make four holes in the base of the trap to match those in the can. Wire the can tightly to the trap, twisting the ends of the wire together under the trap.

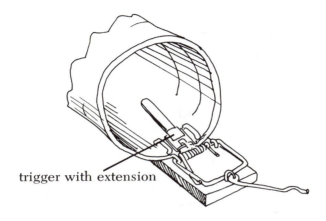

trigger with extension

4. Wire a piece of ¼-inch wire screening to the snap arm of the trap. Or use the can lid, wiring it to the snap arm. Make a hole in the lid for the locking bar.

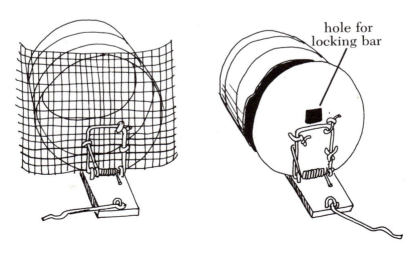

hole for locking bar

3

TREES AND WEEDS

You can do many good projects with the trees and plants that grow in your yard or neighborhood. You could make a collection of tree leaves, tree seeds, twigs and buds, or tree slabs showing rings. You might try some gardening, and raise vegetables, weed flowers, and tree seedlings. Or you could study and preserve nongreen plants such as mushrooms and fungi.

LEAF COLLECTION

People seem to think about leaves mainly in the fall as they change colors. For many, tree leaves are an annual nuisance when they litter lawns and must be raked into piles and taken away.

You can make a leaf collection any time during the summer or early fall. Pick one leaf from each different kind of tree you find. Select leaves that have not been eaten away by insects. Small or medium-sized leaves are easier to handle than larger ones.

The needles of evergreen trees are leaves, too, but their shapes have been modified to prevent water loss and to offer less resistance to winter winds. Collect clusters of needles from pines, spruces, and firs.

One way to identify a tree is to recognize the shape of its leaves. Aspen leaves are somewhat round, apple leaves are oval, and the leaves of a birch have a triangular shape. Other trees have leaves divided into main parts known as *lobes*. The leaves of most maple trees have three lobes. Oaks are characterized by leaves with rounded notches that divide them into numerous parts.

The edges of some tree leaves are scored by *teeth*. Elm leaves have large teeth, while the teeth of willow and wild cherry are quite small.

All leaves have *veins*, which carry the water, carbon dioxide, and minerals needed by leaves to manufacture food. The veins also stiffen the leaf so that the maximum surface is exposed to the sun. The veins of beech and elm leaves are arranged in a featherlike pattern. Maple and oak leaves have veins that branch out like the fingers of your hand.

Your library will have tree guides to help you identify tree leaves.

PRESERVING AND PRINTING LEAVES

After being removed from a tree, leaves very quickly dry out and curl up. Pressing is the easiest way to preserve leaves in their natural shape. Use transparent tape to attach your leaves to sheets of white paper. Stack the sheets on top of one another and weight the pile with several

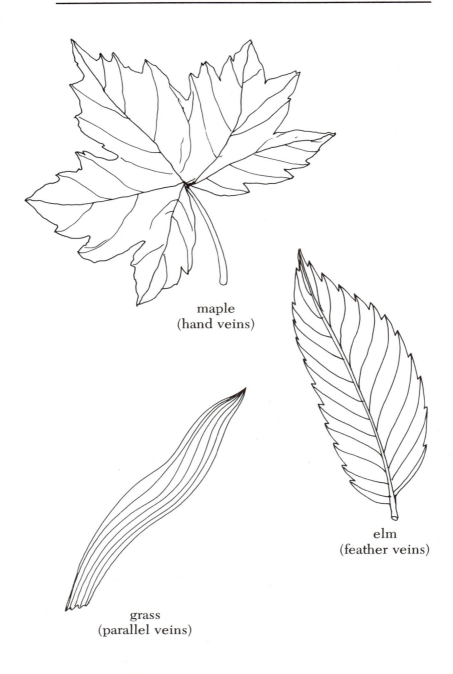

maple
(hand veins)

elm
(feather veins)

grass
(parallel veins)

heavy books. After a few weeks, you can label the dried leaves and put them into a booklet.

Dead leaves are fragile and break apart if bent. However, leaves mounted between two pieces of clear adhesive plastic can be handled without danger of damage. Hardware stores sell transparent adhesive plastic for lining shelves and drawers. Stick the leaves between two pieces of plastic. Then cut around each leaf, leaving a plastic border of about half an inch all the way around.

You can make leaf prints with a dark crayon. Turn a leaf upside down and cover it with a sheet of white paper. Rub the crayon briskly over the paper until the leaf shape has been colored. The leaf's outline and veins should stand out clearly.

How to Spray Leaf Silhouettes

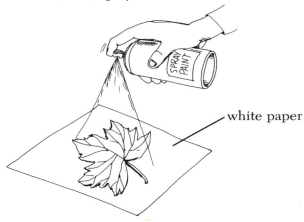

white paper

You can produce leaf silhouettes by placing leaves on clean paper and spraying them with paint from a toothbrush or spray can. A copying machine will make nice leaf prints, too.

WINTER TWIGS

Buds for new tree leaves form even before the old leaves die in the fall. During the winter, cut off the tip of a tree branch and examine its buds. The bud at the outer tip is the *terminal* bud. The smaller buds along the side of the twig are called *lateral* buds. Most tree buds are covered with tough scales to protect the delicate parts inside.

Cut a terminal bud in half crosswise with a sharp knife, and look at it through a magnifying glass. You should be able to see the tightly curled layers of leaves and an embryonic stem for next spring's growth. Although a tree looks bare during the winter, it already has all of its new leaves packed neatly inside the buds.

Just below each bud is a *leaf scar*. The scar marks the spot where the last leaf was attached to the twig. Leaf scars are usually somewhat triangular with a notch at the tip for the new leaf bud. The tiny dots in the scar mark the location of tubes that once supplied the leaf with food and water. Leaf scars on some twigs resemble an animal's face.

Look for wrinkled bands that encircle your twig. Each band is the remains of a former terminal bud. The distance between successive bands shows how much the twig grew each year. In what year did your twig grow fastest? Can you find a twig that is as old as you are?

Take samples of twigs from different kinds of trees and compare them. What tree has the largest terminal buds? Do some trees have buds that are fuzzy or sticky or colored? Are any twigs red or yellow? Are dried fruits or miniature nuts attached to any winter twigs? Even after twigs dry out and shrivel a bit, they retain most of their unique characteristics.

To make a twig label, cut two slits about half an inch apart in a small card. Write identification data on the card and slip the twig through the loop formed by the slits.

You can force the leaves and flowers of trees to bloom before spring if you bring them inside. Twigs that develop well are those from horse chestnut, sumac, cherry, red and silver maple, white ash, and willow. Place the freshly cut twigs in a jar of water. Every three or four days, throw out the old water, shorten the twig slightly by cutting a small piece off the bottom, and put it in fresh water. If this is not done, bacteria and molds might clog the pores and prevent water from traveling up the twig to the buds.

TREE RINGS

A fallen tree or large branch provides an opportunity to study a tree's annual growth rings. Ask an adult to saw off a slab from a fallen tree trunk or branch so you can examine the rings.

Everyone knows that you can find the age of a tree by counting the rings. Most of a tree's growth occurs in the early spring, during the wet, warm months of March and April. The wide part of an annual ring results from the rapid accumulation of wood during this peak growth period. Since a tree grows very little during the rest of the year, the outside of each ring is marked by a thin line.

You should be able to observe other features in your tree slab. The wood toward the center is called *heartwood*, and may be a different color than the outside wood. Sometimes the heartwood rots away, leaving a hole that provides a convenient home for a squirrel, raccoon, or other animal. The growth of a tree takes place in the *cambian* layer, which lies just beneath the bark. If your slab came from a live tree, the cambian layer will be moist and slippery. Older trees have thicker bark, which becomes cracked as the tree continues to increase in size. Tree rings in a branch are off-center and lopsided; the rings are considerably thicker on the bottom than they are on the top.

Annual rings tell much more than a tree's age. The thickness of a ring is a measure of how *much* growth occurred during a particular year. Study the thickness of the annual rings in your tree slab. Can you find some that are unusually narrow or others that are much wider? By counting back, you can figure out which years the tree grew well and in which years it grew poorly.

What could cause variations in a tree's growth rate? Weather is an important factor. A cold, dry March and April would be less favorable than a warm, wet spring. Tree disease and severe insect damage are also reflected in the annual rings. As a tree grows older, other trees might grow up around it, stealing its sunlight and water.

You can make a collection of slabs from different kinds of trees. Cut them all the same size, no more than two inches thick. Sand one side of each slab smooth with sandpaper and give it several coats of clear varnish. Then label the slab to tell the kind of tree and its age.

GROWING TREES FROM SEEDS

There is much variety in the seeds of trees. Sumac trees have bunches of red berries, oaks have acorns, pines have winged seeds inside their cones, and locusts have pods that look like beans.

Gather tree seeds in the fall when they are ripe. Seeds will not sprout if you pull them from the tree before they mature. When the seeds fall to the ground, they are ready for planting.

Start your tree nursery in a plot of ground that receives sun for at least part of the day. Plant the tree seeds about one-half inch deep and mark them with labeled sticks so you know which trees have germinated. You can transplant the seedlings to a permanent location after they have grown for a year or two.

A WEED GARDEN

Weeds often have colorful flowers. You might want to have a weed garden and grow different kinds of weeds you find around your yard or in nearby fields and vacant lots. Give the plants plenty of water for a few weeks after you have transplanted them.

Weeds produce abundant seeds in the fall. Collect flower stalks that still have seeds attached and shake them over the bare earth in part of your garden plot. Roughen the surface of the soil with a rake and then repack it with your feet so the seeds do not blow away.

Some weeds will grow even if they are not planted. Leave a small section of your weed garden unplanted. Watch the weeds that grow there over a period of several years. What kind of weed appears first? How many different kinds of weeds are growing by the second summer?

If you have a microscope, you can examine the pollen from weed flowers. Tap the flower so that its pollen falls on a microscope slide and look at it under low or medium power. Pollen comes in a variety of shapes, sizes, and colors. Compare pollen from different kinds of flowers.

You can plant a flower garden with seeds bought in a garden shop or hardware store. Packets of seeds are available in the spring and are not expensive. You can start the seeds inside during the late winter and plant them outside when the danger of killing frost has passed. There are many beautiful flowers to grow. Sunflowers are fun because they grow so tall and have gigantic yellow flowers.

Seeds sold as food in supermarkets can be grown also. Spices such as mustard seed, celery seed, sesame seed, and caraway seed will germinate. Dried peas, dried beans, and even popcorn will grow if you plant them. Bird seed is a mixture of many kinds of seeds, and it, too, will sprout.

VEGETABLE GARDEN

If you stay at home during the summer, you can raise vegetables. Even in a small garden plot you could grow enough vegetables for tasty meals. Plant the seeds or seedlings early, about the time the grass begins to grow and needs cutting for the first time. Directions for planting are given on the seed packets. If the weather is dry, you should water the small seedlings several times a week. Pull up the weeds that will try to take over your garden. Some of the easiest vegetables to raise are radishes, cucumbers, beans, pumpkins, and squash.

If you raise cucumbers, you can play a trick. Slip a small cucumber into a catsup bottle without breaking it off the main stem. As the cucumber grows, it will become too large to fit through the neck of the bottle. See if people can figure out how you got the cucumber inside the bottle.

Pumpkins and squash grow very quickly in late summer. Measure them with a string and a ruler each day. You will be surprised by their rapid growth.

Your garden will cease growing in late summer as the days become shorter. After harvesting the last vegetables, pull up the plants and pile them in one corner of the garden. You will have a *mulch pile*, which will become organic fertilizer for future gardens. The stems and leaves will slowly rot away, leaving a rich compost that you can spread over your garden next year.

NONGREEN PLANTS

You should be able to find some unusual plants that are not green. Green plants make food from air, water, and minerals, using energy from sunlight. Fungi and mushrooms, however, cannot make their own food and must live on food produced by green plants.

Look for bracket fungi on dead tree trunks and branches. Fungi look like small plates growing out sideways from the tree. Break off several for a display in your room. Fungi come in different shapes, colors, and sizes. Some grow to be almost a foot across, but usually they are somewhat smaller.

Mushrooms live in damp soil that contains rotten vegetation known as *humus*. They develop quickly, sometimes overnight. If you find one, remember to check it daily for growth changes. Since some mushrooms are quite poisonous, you should not pick any.

4

EXPLORATION OF
SPECIAL PLACES

Do you have a pond, ocean, or rock quarry in your backyard? Probably not. Even so, you might live close to an interesting site that you can explore.

A TRIP TO A POND

Most ponds contain abundant life: fish, frogs, turtles, crayfish, water insects, and microscopic protozoa. You might enjoy making a miniature pond in your yard and stocking it with animals you catch.

Making a Pond

A plastic wading pool makes a good artificial pond. Set up your pool in a protected spot in the shade. You could place it under a bush or on an open porch.

The bottom of the pool should be covered with clean gravel. Dirty or dusty gravel must be rinsed before it is used. Put the gravel into a bucket and run a hose into the gravel until the water becomes clear. You can place a few large rocks in the pool to serve as underwater hiding places and above-water resting spots for the animals. Complete your little pond by filling it about halfway with water, using a hose or bucket. Let the water sit a few days to allow any harmful chemicals to escape into the air.

Stocking Your Pond

Nets used for catching water animals are called *dip nets*. You can make a dip net from a large kitchen strainer and a strong pole. Bend back the "ears" of the strainer and flatten the rim in front to change its shape from circular to triangular. Using strong string or plastic tape, lash the handle of the strainer to a long pole.

A fish net, too, can serve as an inexpensive dip net. Pet stores sell fine mesh plastic nets for use by aquarium owners. Sporting goods stores have larger nets for fishing.

You will also need an assortment of plastic containers in which to carry your wildlife home.

The kinds of animals you catch, of course, will depend on what lives in the pond you search. Frogs may be the most universal inhabitants of swamps and ponds. To catch a frog, you need sharp eyes and quick hands. Sneak around the edge of the pond and look for frogs floating in the shallow water or sitting on the bank.

Turtles are almost impossible to catch from the shore. The best technique for capturing turtles is to swim from a boat. You may spot painted turtles sunning themselves on rocks and logs. Even if you approach silently in a boat, however, the tur-

tles will dash back into the water before you can get close enough to net one. You must be prepared to jump overboard and swim underwater in pursuit of the turtle. A face mask and swim fins will improve your chances of making a capture.

Since most fish are much too quick to be caught by hand, you should fish with a rod and a baited hook. Small fish, no more than four inches long, are best for keeping in a nature pool. Fish will live for a while in a bucket of water, but transfer them as soon a possible into your pool.

You can find crayfish on the muddy bottoms of shallow ponds or beneath rocks in streams and lakes. The claws of baby crayfish are too small to hurt you, but you should handle larger ones carefully.

Most of the smaller animals that live in ponds and swamps can be caught easily from the shore with a net. Tadpoles of various sizes rest on the bottom in shallow water. Several kinds of snails and clams live in fresh water. Insects such as dragonfly nymphs, mayfly nymphs, mosquito larvae, diving beetles, and water boatmen hide in the dead vegetation on the bottom. Just scoop up a load of decaying debris in your net and dump it out on the shore. Look for little creatures moving as you pick through the black muck with your fingers.

The only way to see the smallest pond animals is with a microscope. Put a drop of pond water on a microscope and examine it under low power. Can you see anything moving? You might have captured some water fleas, rotifers, waterworms, or one-celled protozoans.

Some water plants will make your pool look more like a real pond. You could collect duckweed, a tiny plant that floats on the surface, and stringy algae clinging to rocks on the bottom. Also, try to dig up a few rooted plants such as water lilies, cattails, water hyacinths, or waterweeds.

Watching Your Pond

You need not worry about feeding the pond animals in your nature pond. Fish, turtles, and frogs are cold-blooded organisms and do not require nearly as much food as warm-blooded birds and mammals. Some of the big animals will eat the smaller animals. Other creatures feed on animals that die or on decaying plants.

You should not attempt to keep the larger animals more than a few weeks, however. Return them to a natural habitat and find new animals to keep in captivity for a while.

Watch the level of the water in your pool. Add more if the level drops because of evaporation loss. Should the rainfall exceed the evaporation rate, you might have to take out some water. Remove dead animals immediately so the water does not become fouled.

Spend time observing the animal activity in your nature pool. Do the fish always stay in the same place? How often does your frog perch on the rock island? How long can the turtle hold its breath underwater? Do the animals try to eat the water insects? Use a flashlight to see how the animals' behavior differs at night.

A TRIP TO THE OCEAN

If you are near the ocean, you can put salt water into the wading pool instead of fresh water. Then you can collect sea animals at low tide and keep them alive in your little ocean.

Make a Mini-Ocean

It is especially important to keep the sea water as cool as possible, since the ocean does not warm up very much during the summer. The pool must be kept in a place that is in the shade all day. If the pool is sunk into the ground, the soil will help insulate the water from the warmer air.

Put beach sand on the bottom of the pool, and add a few large rocks to provide hiding places for the animals.

Collect sea water in plastic milk jugs or buckets. Put a trash bag in the bucket before filling it with water. The sea water will not slosh out of the bucket if you fold the plastic over the water's surface. Fill the pool almost to the top, since a larger volume of water will not warm up as quickly during the daytime.

Stocking Your Ocean

The best time to collect animals is at low tide. If you can find a shore with rocks, tide pools containing sea animals will be left behind as the water recedes. You can also find some animals on mud flats left exposed when the tide is out.

Do not attempt to keep too many animals in your saltwater pool. If the pool is crowded, the oxygen supply in the water will be exhausted too quickly, causing many of the animals to die. There should be about three gallons of water for each animal in captivity.

The first animals you find in tide pools probably will be those that do not hide. A sea urchin clings to rocks with hundreds of tube feet, and you may have to pry it loose with a stick. You can use your hands, but do not squeeze the urchin too hard. Sea urchin spines are not poisonous, but they are sharp enough to stick into your skin.

Starfish, too, might hide on underwater rocks. Collect a few medium-sized specimens; it is more difficult to keep large animals alive.

Sea Life Specimens

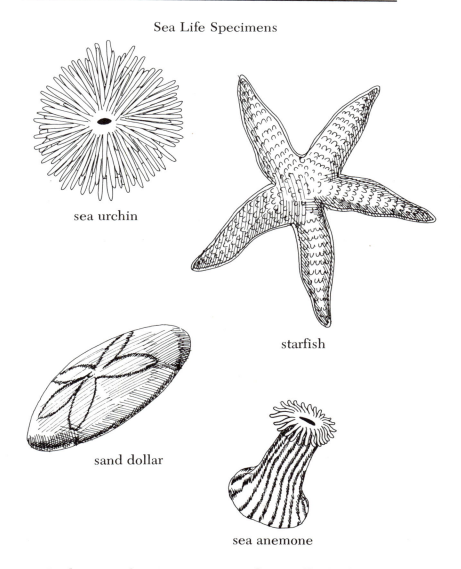

sea urchin

starfish

sand dollar

sea anemone

Crabs are shy creatures, and usually hide under rocks. Turn over loose rocks and look for crabs underneath. The rocks do not even have to be in the water, since crabs can live in moist air until the tide comes back in. If you grab a crab by the back of its shell where the legs attach, it will not nip your hand. Eels, too, are sometimes discovered beneath small rocks.

You do not need a net to collect animals from the ocean shore. Your hands are the best tools. Take along a few plastic containers with snap tops in which to carry the animals back to your pool.

Sea anemones can be found only in tide pools exposed during very low tide. An anemone looks like a fat flower, with a soft body and tentacles around the top. You will need a knife to cut the base of the anemone away from the rock. The animal will close up into a little ball, but it should puff up and spread out its tentacles after you place it in your saltwater pool.

Some sea animals found less frequently are brittlestars, sea squirts, jellyfish, sea slugs, sponges, and sand shrimps.

There are some very common animals that you should not overlook. Mussels and periwinkles usually grow in abundance in rocky coastal areas. Barnacles attach themselves to rocks too firmly to be removed. Instead, find a smaller rock covered with barnacles and place the whole thing in your mini-ocean.

A few animals can be found at low tide in the shallow water of sandy or muddy shorelines. You can wade in or have someone row you around in a boat. Here a long-handled net would be useful to retrieve sand dollars and hermit crabs from the bottom.

A few plants will make your sea-life pool more attractive and also provide food for some of the animals. You might find kelp, rockweed, Irish moss, and sea lettuce attached to small rocks.

Do not transfer animals directly from the ocean

into your saltwater pool. Sudden temperature changes will kill many kinds of animals. Hold the newly captured animals in the plastic carrying containers for several hours until the sea water warms up, and then transfer them into the pool.

Crabs are pugnacious bullies and often eat sea urchins, periwinkles, and smaller crabs. For this reason, you might want to isolate your crabs in one part of the pool. Roll a piece of window screening into a large cylinder and place it in the tank. Put the crabs inside the cage, but cover the top with a board so they cannot climb over.

Care and Feeding of Ocean Life

Feed your ocean animals infrequently. Once or twice a week you could drop in a mussel that has been cracked open or a small portion of frozen fish from the supermarket. Place bits of food on the sea urchin's spines and in the sea anemone's mouth at the center of the tentacles. Remove all uneaten food in a few hours so it does not rot and pollute the water. Starfish will eat the barnacles and mussels, while periwinkles feed on algae growing on seaweeds.

Watch the animals so you can learn about their anatomy, locomotion, and behavior. Do the crabs ever swim? What parts of a crab stick out of the sand when it is buried? How do sea urchins move? What does a barnacle look like when it is feeding? Where do the starfish stay in the pool? Turn a starfish over on its back and watch it get right-side up again.

After you have kept your sea animals for a few weeks, return them to their home in the ocean.

ROCK-COLLECTING TRIPS

You can find rocks and minerals almost everywhere. By collecting rocks during your weekend travels and summer vacations, you can make an interesting collection. In addition to minerals you find, you could purchase a few nice specimens at museum gift shops.

You need only a few supplies for rock collecting. A sturdy bag is necessary for carrying rocks. A canvas day pack is fine; paper and plastic bags are almost useless since they tear easily.

You also should have a hammer to break apart rocks to look for minerals inside. You can pound a cold chisel with an ordinary carpentry hammer. A prospector's pick is made especially for rock collecting; it has a tapered head with a point on the back. Always wear protective glasses or goggles when hammering.

You could begin a collection with rocks found around your house and school. Pebbles in the soil might be quartz, granite, or shale. Sometimes crushed stone from quarries is used for driveways and paths. When workers begin a new building, they usually dig rocks out of the ground from the foundation hole.

Be alert for places to gather rocks as you travel. You can find smooth, colorful pebbles in stream beds and along the shores of lakes and oceans. Deep layers of rocks are exposed on cliffs left by highway construction. Ask the driver to stop the car so you can run out and pick up a few samples.

Abandoned mines and quarries are some of the best places to find unusual rocks and minerals. Ask people who know the area to direct you to promising spots. At the mine, pick through piles of rubble that have been dumped near the excavation site. Look along dirt roads in the area, too. Always seek permission of the owner if you collect on private property.

Specimens in a good mineral collection are marked with numbers for identification. Perhaps the neatest way is to use the little disks that are punched out of paper with a paper punch. Glue a disk to each rock with a drop of wood glue, and write a number on the disk after the glue dries. Keep a numbered list that tells where you found each rock and what its name is.

Rocks are difficult to identify, since the same kind can have a variety of appearances. A field guide with color photographs of rocks and minerals is essential. Many museums have beautiful displays of common and rare minerals.

The properties of a mineral are the key to its identification. Color is an obvious characteristic. Coal is jet black, while limestone is usually white or gray. The same mineral can have different colors. Quartz, for example, can be clear, white, pink, or dark gray.

The hardness of a mineral is rated on a scale from 0 to 10. Gypsum is a soft rock with a hardness of 2, while quartz has a hardness of 7. You can use a clear plastic container, a tin can, and a glass jar to obtain a rough measure of hardness. Plastic is soft, steel has a medium hardness, and glass is very hard. Try to scratch the three materials with the mineral you are testing. Mica is so soft that it will not scratch the plastic, but quartz is hard enough to scratch glass.

Soft rocks often leave a streak when they are rubbed on a piece of unglazed white tile. You should be able to get a few pieces of unglazed bathroom tile at a tile store. Rub the mineral on the tile and see if it makes a colored streak. Anthracite coal and obsidian are both shiny black, yet only the coal leaves a black streak.

Many minerals occur in crystal form. Quartz has six-sided crystals that terminate in a point. The

CRYSTALS

DOGTOOTH CALCITE   AMETHYST

GEODES

MINERALS   MUSCOVI

STALAGTITE

A rock collection with the specimens labeled.

cubic crystals of halite and galena look like little boxes. Use a magnifying glass to examine any crystals you pry from rock crevices.

You might want to display your rock collection in your bedroom. You could arrange your best minerals on a bookshelf or make a special display case out of wood.

COLLECTION OF
DAVID OSGOOD
DEXTER SCHOOL

FOSSILS

ROCKS

SHELL

SHARK TOOTH

GRANITE

COQUINA

OYSTER

RED SHALE

UNKNOWN

FISH

TRILOBITE

5

A BACKYARD
WEATHER WATCH

Everyone talks about the weather, but very few people are able to predict it. By watching weather signs and making some simple measurements, you can become a good short-range weather forecaster.

Some instruments can measure temperature, air pressure, rainfall, wind, and humidity. It's a good idea to become familiar with these weather instruments before you try to make predictions.

WEATHER INSTRUMENTS

You can buy a weather station that includes a hygrometer, thermometer, barometer, rain gauge, anemometer, and wind-speed indicator, but this will be quite expensive. You can make or buy most of your own instruments for relatively little cost. The ones you will need are listed below.

Thermometer

Perhaps your family already has an outdoor thermometer. If not, you can purchase one relatively cheaply. Hang the thermometer in a shady place that is well away from your house or apartment and several feet above the ground. Read the thermometer several times a day and record the temperature on a chart like the one at the end of this section.

Barometer

You can also purchase a barometer, the instrument that measures atmospheric pressure. Or you might ask your science teacher to help you make a Cape Cod barometer. The Cape Cod barometer shown in the drawing responds to temperature as

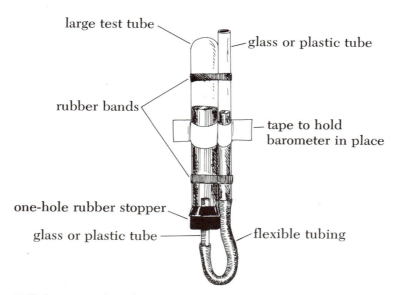

large test tube

glass or plastic tube

rubber bands

tape to hold barometer in place

one-hole rubber stopper

glass or plastic tube

flexible tubing

Fill the test tube about two-thirds full. Put in rubber stopper with attached tubing. Invert. Blow gently into end of tube to force liquid from test tube into tubing. To see effects of change in air pressure on liquid level in tubing, blow air very gently into tubing or carefully suck air from end of tubing.

well as pressure, so you should try to keep this barometer in a place where temperature changes are minimal. If you buy an aneroid barometer, which is more reliable, see what happens to the pressure when you take the barometer for a ride in a car. As you will find, a barometer can be used as an altimeter, the instrument that gives the height of a location above sea level.

Rain Gauge

A rain gauge is used to determine the depth of rainwater that collects during a twenty-four-hour period or during a storm. You can make the rain gauge shown in the drawing. It has a funnel so that you can collect more rain than would fall into the narrower vial or jar. This allows you to measure rainfall more accurately.

A Rain Gauge

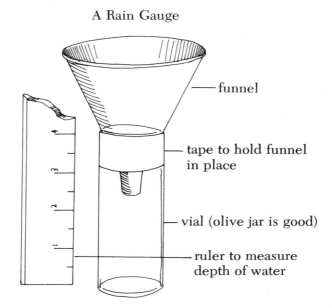

funnel

tape to hold funnel in place

vial (olive jar is good)

ruler to measure depth of water

To find the actual rainfall, measure the change in the depth of water in the vial. Next, find the ratio of the diameter of the funnel to the diameter of the vial. Square this ratio. Then divide the water depth in the vial by the square of the ratio to find the rainfall in inches.

For example, suppose you find 1 inch of water collected in the vial during one day. If the vial has a diameter of 1 inch and the funnel a diameter of 2 inches, the ratio is 2. The square of 2 is 4. The actual rainfall was, therefore, 1 inch ÷ 4 = ¼ inch of rain.

Why must the diameter ratio be squared in order to find the rainfall?

A Hygrometer

With a hygrometer you can measure *relative humidity,* the percentage of water actually dissolved in the air as compared to the maximum amount that could be dissolved at the same temperature.

To make such an instrument, tape two identical thermometers side by side on a thin board that has been securely attached to a firm support in a shady place. Let the bulbs extend beyond the board so that air can circulate around them. To one thermometer add an absorbent cloth wick. Attach one end of the wick to the bulb with a rubber band. Let the other end dip into a small container of water. When the bulb and wick are wet, you will observe a decrease in the temperature of the wet bulb because water on the wick evaporates. When the temperature stops falling, read both thermometers.

Table of Relative Humidity

Difference between dry-bulb and wet-bulb temperatures in degrees Fahrenheit

Dry-bulb temp	1	2	3	4	5	6	7	8	9	10	11	12	14	16	18	20	22	24	26	28	30	32	34
10	78	56	34	13																			
15	82	64	46	29	11																		
20	85	70	55	40	26	12																	
25	87	74	62	49	37	25	13	1															
30	89	78	67	56	46	36	26	16	6														
35	91	81	72	63	54	45	36	27	19	10	2												
40	92	83	75	68	60	52	45	37	29	22	15	7											
45	93	86	78	71	64	57	51	44	38	31	25	18	6										
50	93	87	80	74	67	61	55	49	43	38	32	27	16	5									
55	94	88	82	76	70	65	59	54	49	43	38	33	23	14	5								
60	94	89	83	78	73	68	63	58	53	48	43	39	30	21	13	5							
65	95	90	85	80	75	70	66	61	56	52	48	44	35	27	20	12	5						
70	95	90	86	81	77	72	68	64	59	55	51	48	40	33	25	19	12	6					
75	96	91	86	82	78	74	70	66	62	58	54	51	44	37	30	24	18	12	7	1			
80	96	91	87	83	79	75	72	68	64	61	57	54	47	41	35	29	23	18	12	7	3		
90	96	92	89	85	81	78	74	71	68	65	61	58	52	47	41	36	31	26	22	17	13	9	5
100	96	93	89	86	83	80	77	73	70	68	65	62	56	51	46	41	37	33	28	24	21	17	13

Dry-bulb temperature, degrees Fahrenheit

Find the difference between the wet and dry bulb temperatures. Then, using the table, determine the relative humidity. Find the temperature closest to the dry bulb temperature at the left of the table. Move your finger to the right, stopping at the column where the number at the top is the difference between dry and wet bulb temperatures. The number where the row and column meet is the relative humidity expressed as a percent.

For example, if the dry bulb temperature is 60 degrees and the difference between the dry and wet bulb temperatures is 5 degrees, the relative humidity is 73 percent.

Wind Vane

Ask an adult to help you make a simple wind vane like the one shown in the drawing. When

A Wind Vane

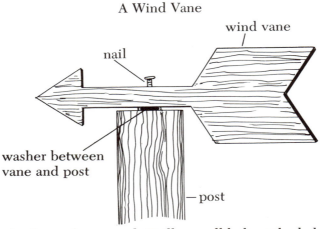

Cut the figure from wood. Drill a small hole at the balance point. A nail through the hole will connect vane to post. Use a washer to reduce friction.

you place it in an open area, the arrow will point toward the direction from which the wind is blowing.

A *Wind-Speed Meter*

The wind-speed meter shown in the drawing can also be built quite easily with a little adult help. You can mark the speed settings on the meter by holding it outside the window of a car moving through still air. The little flap will move higher as the wind increases. Label the position of the flap at various wind speeds as indicated by the car's speedometer. Then nail up the board outside.

A Wind-Speed Meter

one-inch strip of metal cut from can. Fold one end and hang on top nail.

nails

board

50
40
30
10 20

Calibrate by holding meter outside the window of a car moving at known speed.

CLOUD CLUES

All clouds are tiny droplets of water or ice crystals that form because the temperature at the altitude of the clouds is below the dew point. The

Cirrus clouds.

Stratus clouds.

dew point is the temperature at which moisture in the air condenses.

Careful observations of clouds can help you to become a competent weather forecaster. There are three types of clouds—cirrus, stratus, and cumulus.

Cirrus clouds are thin, streaky, wispy clouds that have a feathery appearance. They are high clouds (above 20,000 feet) consisting of ice crystals. Such clouds indicate fair weather unless they thicken. When these high clouds form small white puffs, they are called cirrocumulus. Extensive cirrocumulus clouds create what is called a mackerel sky. A mackerel sky accompanied by lower, thicker clouds may indicate precipitation within a day's time.

Cirrus clouds that form a thin, sheetlike cover on the sky are called cirrostratus clouds. They often produce a halo around the sun or moon. The halo is caused by light reflected from small ice crystals in the clouds. If a halo persists, rain is likely within a day.

Stratus clouds are flat and layered. Fog is a stratus cloud that is close to the ground. At higher levels these clouds may produce a hazy sky and light drizzle if they thicken. Thick layers of stratus clouds are called nimbostratus and are usually associated with steady precipitation.

Cumulus clouds look like tufts of cotton against a clear blue sky. They are often called fair-weather clouds. However, cumulus clouds may swell and grow upward, producing the huge thunderheads that precede a thunderstorm.

Cumulus clouds.

WEATHER CHARTS

To learn to forecast weather you should keep a record of rainfall during a twenty-four-hour period. Also observe temperature, wind, clouds, air pressure, and so forth. Note things that occur before a weather change occurs. Record the data each day at the same time or times. Make a chart like the sample shown here.

Weather Observations

Date	7/4/86
Time	10:30 A.M.
Temperature	80F
Wind speed	5mph
Wind direction	West
Cloud cover	◑ (partly cloudy)
	● (cloudy)
	O (clear)
Cloud type	Cumulus
Rain or snow	0.20 in.
Rel. Humidity	45%
Air pressure	29.6 in.
Comments	Wind shift to W from S

FORECASTING THE WEATHER

After you have collected weather data for a while, you may be ready to try your hand at forecasting. Don't be discouraged if you're not terribly accurate at first. It requires experience. Even professional weather forecasters make accurate forecasts no more than 70 percent of the time.

If you watch TV weather forecasts, you will notice that, in general, weather patterns move from west to east. So if you know the weather to your west today, you can often predict the weather you will have tomorrow.

Here are some forecasting indicators offered by other amateur forecasters. See if they agree with your observations at this point.

- A wind from the east, together with falling air pressure, indicates an approaching storm.
- A shift of the wind to the west indicates the approach of fair weather.
- Winds from the south or southwest, accompanied by a steady decrease in air pressure, indicate a storm approaching from the west or northwest.
- A steadily falling air pressure, accompanied by winds from the east or northeast, indicates a storm is coming from the south or southwest.
- You can expect a storm when
    A. there is a halo around the moon or sun,
    B. the air pressure falls steadily,
    C. clouds thicken and darken,
    D. low-level clouds move in from the south or east at high speed,
    E. the wind shifts to the south or east,
    F. the temperature rises abruptly as damp air moves in from the south or east,
    G. after several days of wind from the west or north, the wind speed drops at sunset and the sun sets behind cirrus clouds.
- You can expect the weather to clear when
    A. clouds break up and patches of blue sky appear,

    B. the wind shifts to the west or north,
    C. the air pressure rises rapidly,
    D. the cloud base rises.

■ You can expect continued fair weather when
    A. the air pressure is steady or rising,
    B. the temperature is steady and seasonally normal,
    C. fog or stratus clouds seem to be burning off after sunrise,
    D. the wind continues to blow from the west,
    E. the sun sets in a clear sky,
    F. there is dew or frost at night.

■ You can expect colder weather when
    A. the wind shifts to the north or northwest,
    B. a west wind diminishes at night and the sun sets in a clear sky,
    C. the air pressure increases,
    D. clouds break up and the northern sky has a greenish tint.

■ You can expect warmer weather when
    A. it's cloudy at night,
    B. a northwest wind diminishes and later blows from the south.

As you continue to collect data and forecast weather, you might enjoy collecting some wet weather.

PRESERVING SNOWFLAKES

On a cold snowy day place several microscope slides or glass plates on a flat sheet of wood or cardboard. Put the sheet with slides in a cold but protected place such as an unheated garage, a freezer, or outdoors in a covered box. At the same time, put a spray can of clear lacquer (the aerosol lacquer Krylon works well) in a cold place, too.

When the glass and lacquer have cooled to a point well below freezing, spray a thin coat of lacquer on each piece of glass. Then carry the sheet of slides into the falling snow. Be careful not to let your warm hands touch the slides. After a few flakes have settled on each slide, place the sheet back in its protected cold place. Leave it for several hours, until the lacquer is thoroughly dry.

The lacquer will coat the snowflakes and preserve their shapes. You can then examine them with a microscope or magnifier.

Keeps a record of how long these snowflakes remain preserved.

What shape do the snowflakes have? Do they all have the same shape? Do snowflakes from a different storm have a different appearance? Can you preserve sleet in the same way? How can you preserve frost patterns like those that form on winter windowpanes?

CATCH A FALLING RAINDROP

You can capture and preserve raindrops by letting them fall into a pan of fine flour. The flour should be at least one inch deep so that the drops do not splatter. Each drop will form a small pellet of dough. Just a few seconds' exposure to a steady rain will provide plenty of drops.

When the pellets are dry, you can measure their diameters. But do the pellets have the same size as the drops that formed them? Probably not, but you can produce drops of known size, let them fall into flour, and measure the pellets formed.

To produce drops of known size, let drops form at the ends of various eyedroppers, drawn-glass tubes, or capillary tubes. To determine the size of the drops, find the volume of a hundred or more and divide to find the volume of one.

In a gentle rain you may be able to capture the drops on waxed paper supported by a cookie pan or cardboard sheet. Watch to be sure the drops don't splatter when they land.

Do the sizes of raindrops vary? Do the sizes change as a storm continues? Are winter raindrops larger than summer raindrops? Are drops from a steady rain smaller than those from a shower? How many snowflakes does it take to make an average raindrop? How many inches of snow are required to make an inch of rain?

HOW FAR AWAY IS THE STORM?

Because the speed of light (186,000 miles per second) is so much greater than the speed of sound (about 1/5 mile per second), you can assume that the time required for a lightning flash to reach your eyes is practically zero. If you count the number of seconds between the time you see lightning and the moment you hear the thunder it produces, you can approximate the distance to the storm. Since sound travels 1/5 mile per second, dividing the time you measured by 5 will give you the distance to the storm in miles.

For example, if you hear the thunder 4 seconds after you see the lightning flash, the storm is about 4/5 mile away.

By repeating this experiment every few minutes, you can tell whether the storm is approaching or moving away. If the storm is approaching, seek shelter. Never stay outside in a thunderstorm if you can avoid it.

INSECT BROADCASTERS

Some people claim that crickets "broadcast" the temperature. Listen to a cricket and count the number of times it chirps in 14 seconds. Make several counts and average them. Add 40 to your average count and you will have the temperature in degrees Fahrenheit, according to some people. Others say you should add 50.

Do you agree with either group?

WEATHER POEMS

As an experienced weather forecaster, do you find any truth to these poems?

Red sky at morning,
Sailors take warning;
Red sky at night,
Sailors' delight.

If the moon shows a silver shield,
Be not afraid to reap your fields;
But if the moon rises haloed 'round,
Soon we'll tread on rainy ground

Now write your own weather poem based on what you have learned about weather.

6

LIGHT AND SHADOWS
IN THE BACKYARD
OR ON THE ROOF

When sunlight, moonlight, or the light from a street lamp falls on your yard, apartment rooftop, park, or playground, it casts shadows. (If you go to a rooftop, get permission from a parent first. Be sure that there are guard rails around the roof and do not lean out over them.) In addition to your own shadow, you may see shadows of sticks, posts, houses, animals, people, and maybe even the shadow of a passing cloud, bird, or airplane.

SHADOWS TO TELL TIME AND SEASON

Watch the shadow of a vertical stick or pole, or the shadow cast by a house or building at frequent intervals during the course of an entire day. What happens to the length of the shadow between early morning and midday? Between noon and sunset? In what direction does the shadow "point" at sunrise? At midday? At sunset? If you don't know the directions (north, east, south, west) around your home, use a magnetic compass. The marked end of the needle will point in a northerly direction, though probably not directly toward the North Pole.

Use a camera or some other recording method to mark the direction of the shadow shortly after sunrise and just before sunset.

Watch the shadow of the same stick, pole, or building throughout the day at various times of the year. Again, a camera will help you keep a permanent record of the shadows. The beginnings of the four seasons would be appropriate times to choose. A good calendar will reveal that the seasons begin on or near the twenty-first day of four months: March, June, September, and December. In North America the sun rises in the direction due east and sets in the direction due west at the beginning of spring and autumn (about March 21 and September 21). In what direction does the sun rise and set at the start of summer? At the start of winter? Does the sun always rise in the east and set in the west?

What do you notice about midday shadows?

The photograph of the house on the next pages was taken from the west side. At what time of day was it taken? At what time of the year?

A SUNDIAL

There are many types of sundials, some of them very old. None of them keep as perfect time as a clock. However, the one described below will keep reasonably good time.

A square piece of plywood 12 inches on a side

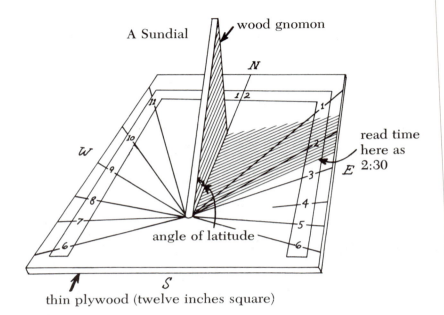

A Sundial

wood gnomon

N

W

E

read time here as 2:30

angle of latitude

S

thin plywood (twelve inches square)

can serve as the base for your sundial. You can cut a gnomon (see drawing) from a thin piece of plywood or sheet metal (ask an adult to help you). The angle of the south end of the gnomon should equal the latitude of the earth where you live. You can find the latitude of your town by looking at a map or a globe. Glue the gnomon to the base or insert it into a slot cut in the base. Be sure the slot is the same width as the gnomon.

You can use the sun to help you mark hour lines on the base of the sundial. Place the instrument on a level surface that will be in sunlight all day, a place where the dial can be left permanently. At midday according to the sun (about noon, standard clock time), the sun will be near due south. Actually, midday according to the sun may vary by as much as fifteen minutes according to a clock. But from April to mid-September the variation between sun time and clock time will not exceed five minutes.

When it is twelve o'clock standard time (one o'clock daylight saving time), turn the sundial until the gnomon casts the narrowest shadow possible. Draw a line down the center of the shadow and label it with the time of day ("12" or "1"). Mark succeeding lines at one-hour intervals by drawing lines along the edge of the shadow cast by the sloping edge of the gnomon. Mark the second line "1" or "2." Repeat this procedure at hourly intervals until sunset.

To finish calibrating your dial, measure the angle between the noon line and the 1:00 P.M. line. The line that indicates 11:00 A.M. will have the same angle to the left of the noon line; 10:00 A.M. will have the same angle as 2:00 P.M., and so on.

You can decorate your sundial using durable paint so that it can be left outside in one place permanently.

NIGHT SHADOWS

Stand near a porch light or street lamp at night. Try to predict what will happen to your shadow as you walk away from the light. Were you right? What happens to your shadow as you walk toward the light?

On a moonlit night you will have two shadows if you stand near a porch light or street lamp. Why do you have two shadows? See if you can predict which shadow will change its length as you walk. Which shadow can you make dimmer? How could you cast three shadows?

SHARP AND FUZZY SHADOWS

Look at the shadow of a tall stick, pole, or flag-pole early in the morning or late in the afternoon. The part of the shadow at the bottom of the pole or stick is quite sharp and distinct. But toward the outer end, the edges of the shadow become fuzzy and lighter. Why do you think the shadow gets fuzzier when farther from the object that casts the shadow? The experiment described below may help you answer this question.

It's dangerous to look directly at the sun because it can damage your eyes. But you can look at the moon. When a nearly full moon or a street lamp is casting a long shadow of a stick or pole, place your eye in the shadow and look at the moon or light. First, look up toward the light source with your eye in the center of the shadow close to the pole; then look toward the light with your eye in the shadow far from the pole. What is different as you view the moon or light from these two places? Now can you explain why the end of the shadow was fuzzy?

A MIRROR IN THE SUN

Take a mirror to your yard, park, roof, or playground. Notice how you can reflect sunlight onto a building, a tree, or the ground. Be careful not to reflect sunlight into someone's eyes. The sun's rays can do serious damage to eyes. When the sun is to the right of the mirror, where do you find the reflected beam?

Have someone "capture" a beam of reflected light from your mirror on a sheet of cardboard. You will see that the shape of the reflected spot is the same as that of the mirror. But as the screen is moved farther from the mirror, what happens to the shape of the reflected spot? Why do you think this happens?

PINHOLE IMAGES OF THE SUN

Make a screen by taping a sheet of white paper to a piece of cardboard. Use a pin to punch a small hole in the center of a sheet of dark construction paper. Hold the screen under the hole in the dark paper so that sunlight shines through the hole onto the screen. You are seeing an image of the sun. What happens to the size of the image as you move the screen closer to and then farther from the pinhole? See if you can explain how the image is formed.

What do you think will happen if you punch a second pinhole in the paper? A third hole? Try it!

What happens to the image if you make the hole a little bigger? If you make a very tiny hole?

In a second sheet of black paper cut very small round, square, and triangular holes. You can do this quite easily by folding the paper and cutting half a circle, half a square, and half a triangle at the fold. Does the shape of the hole affect the shape of the sun's image if you hold the screen a foot or more from the holes?

To get a better look at the sun's image, cut a small square near the bottom of one of the narrow sides of a large, long, narrow box. A box about 1 foot by 4 feet by 4 feet would be good, but any large box will do. Cover the hole with black paper and punch a tiny pinhole in the center of the paper. Tape a sheet of white paper on the side of the box opposite the pinhole. Invert the box and put your head inside so you can see the pinhole image of the sun in semidarkness. By measuring the diameter of the sun's image and the length of the box, and knowing that the sun is 94 million miles away, see if you can figure out a way to determine the diameter of the sun.

On a bright, sunny summer day look at the round patches of light within the shadow cast by a tree's leaves. These, too, are pinhole images of the sun. Can you figure out what made them?

A PINHOLE CAMERA

If you know how to develop film, you might enjoy taking some pictures with a pinhole camera. You'll need a light-tight box and a way to mount or tape film at one end of the box. At the other end of the box you can punch a tiny pinhole. Cover the pinhole with tape. Take the box into a dark place and load the film. Then take the camera outside. Point the pinhole camera at the subject you want to photograph and uncover the pinhole for several minutes. Be sure the camera does not move while the pinhole is uncovered. Then remove the film and develop it. You can experiment with different exposure times until you find how long it takes to get good pictures under different light conditions. What will happen to the required exposure time if you enlarge the pinhole? What will happen to the quality of the picture?

CAMERA EXPERIMENTS

If you're a beginning photographer, you might like to experiment with your camera. First choose a subject to photograph. Then, keeping everything else the same, take a series of pictures using different aperture sizes (f-stops). Repeat the experiment, but this time keep everything the same except the shutter speed. Finally, repeat the experiment using film with different ASA values. Keep a careful record of your experiments so that you'll know which picture is associated with each f-stop, shutter speed, and film speed.

What is the effect of changing the aperture opening? The shutter speed? The film speed?

COLORS FROM THE SUN

Using the same box you used to see the sun's image, remove the paper with the pinhole. Cover the square hole with a diffraction grating—a square about two inches on a side that has thousands of fine parallel scratches ruled in the clear plastic. You can buy such a grating from a hobby shop or one of the science supply companies listed in the Appendix, or you might be able to borrow one from your school. Let sunlight come through the grating while you watch the white screen from within the box. Off to each side of the bright patch of light coming through the square grating you will see all the colors of the rainbow. If you don't see this spectrum of colors, turn the grating 90 degrees and look again.

You can break sunlight into colors in other ways, too. One way is with a prism, a triangular piece of glass or plastic. Hold the prism in a beam of sunlight. On a screen held to one side of the prism you will see a spectrum of colors. You may have to turn the prism and move the screen to get the best spectrum possible.

You can even make your own rainbow. Have someone spray water from the fine nozzle opening of a garden hose. If you view the water with the sun at your back, you will be able to see the rainbow of colors coming from light reflected from within the droplets. This is what causes a real rainbow. Raindrops form millions of tiny "prisms" that bend light and then reflect it to your eyes.

SOLAR HEATING

To show that you can get heat from the sun, place a thermometer on a sheet of cardboard. Fasten the thermometer to the cardboard with a strip of masking tape placed over the bulb. Put the thermometer in a shady place. When the thermometer's temperature is steady, put it in bright sunlight. What happens to the temperature?

With a small magnifying glass you can concentrate sunlight on your hand. What happens to the temperature when you focus the sunlight to a small area on your hand?

Have you ever noticed how warm you feel when you wear dark clothing in sunlight? It's not by accident that people in warm countries often wear white clothing. To see the difference for yourself, cover the bulbs of several thermometers with equal-size sheets (about 2 inches × 4 inches) of different-colored construction paper. Use black, white, and several bright colors. Fold the paper about each thermometer in the same way. You can use a paper clip to hold the paper in place.

Place the thermometers side by side on an insulating sheet of cardboard. Record the temperature inside each color before placing the thermometers in bright sunlight. Note the temperature within each colored sheet at one-minute intervals for about fifteen minutes. Which color seems to be the best absorber of heat? Which seems to be the best reflector of heat?

Obtain two identical aluminum pie pans. Paint one pan with flat black paint. When the paint has dried, pour equal amounts of water into both pans. Place the pans on an insulating sheet of cardboard in a warm, sunny place. See if you can predict which pan will convert more of the sunlight into heat. How can you test your prediction?

Instead of painting the pans, you might use food coloring or ink to darken the water. Which color absorbs more solar energy? Which do you think will absorb more solar energy for the same volume—apple juice or grape juice?

7

BACKYARD ASTRONOMY

Try to find an open space in your yard, park, playground, or rooftop where you can observe as much of the sky as possible. This place should be dark at night so that house or street lights do not interfere with your ability to see the stars clearly. Look up at the sky as you stand in this dark place. You are at the very center of a huge dark dome. Astronomers call this dome the *celestial hemisphere*.

FINDING TRUE NORTH

As you may know, true north, the direction to the North Pole, is not usually the same direction as magnetic north. To find true north, push a stick or pencil into the ground so it sticks straight up. Do this late in the morning. Draw a circle around the stick, using its shadow as a radius. Use a pebble to mark the position of the shadow on the circle. The shadow will move and shorten as midday approaches. Then it will lengthen. When the shadow again touches the circle, place another pebble at that point. Connect the pebbles with a straight line. A line from the stick to the center of the line connecting the pebbles will point true north.

The shortest shadow may not occur at twelve noon (standard time). Midday according to clock and sun usually differ. If you live in Bangor, Maine, and you call someone in Detroit, Michigan, you will both agree that it is the same time according to the clock because you both live in time zone 5. If it's midday in Bangor, the sun will be due south. However, at this same time in Detroit, which is farther west, the sun still has an hour to go before it will be due south.

To confirm that the mark you have made on the ground points north, see if it is aligned with the North Star (Polaris). You can find the North Star at night by first locating the *Big Dipper* in the northern sky. Depending on the hour and the season, the dipper may be turned in various ways or even partially hidden. You should be able to find the two stars (Dubhe and Merak) that form one end of the dipper (opposite the handle) as shown in the drawing. At arm's length put your

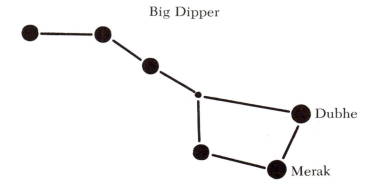

Big Dipper

Dubhe

Merak

thumb on one of these two stars and your index finger on the other. Using Merak and Dubhe to form an imaginary line and your thumb and finger to measure the distance between the same two stars, extend the line a little more than five times the distance between the two stars. You will come to Polaris, the North Star, a star of only moderate brightness. It is almost directly above earth's North Pole, and it marks the tip of the handle of the *Little Dipper*.

The altitude of the North Star, the angle be-

Cassiopeia

Little Dipper

Polaris

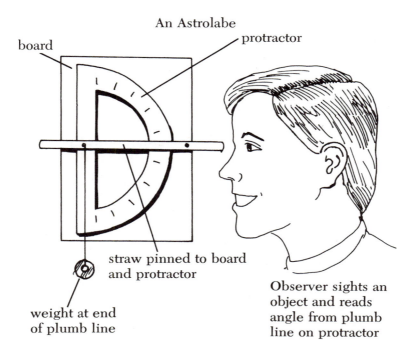

An Astrolabe

board

protractor

straw pinned to board
and protractor

weight at end
of plumb line

Observer sights an
object and reads
angle from plumb
line on protractor

tween the star and the horizon, is equal to your
latitude on earth. To make an approximate test,
hold your clenched fist at arm's length. Align the
top of your fist with the horizon below the North
Star. Then find how many fists it takes to reach
Polaris. A fist is very nearly ten degrees. (You'll
find that nine fists, one on top of the other, take
you from the horizon to a point directly above
you.) Look at a globe or map to find your latitude
on earth.

To measure altitudes more accurately, you can
make an astrolabe as shown in the drawing.

OTHER CONSTELLATIONS

A group of stars in the sky that form a pattern is
called a constellation. You have found two con-

stellations, the Big Dipper and the Little Dipper. Another constellation, Cassiopeia, is easy to find in the northern sky. It lies on the opposite side of the Little Dipper from the Big Dipper. Some people see it as a lazy W; to others it looks like a dentist's chair.

Try to observe these three constellations over a period of several hours. If you wake up during the night, take another look. What happens to these stars as the night progresses?

What do you notice about the location of these three constellations as the seasons change? Do you always find the Big Dipper in the same position at the same time each night of the year? What about the North Star? How can you explain what you observe?

If you have a camera, point it directly at Polaris and leave the shutter open for about thirty minutes without moving the camera. What do you find when the film is developed? You may want to try a variety of exposure times, f-stops, and film speeds until you get satisfactory pictures. Try color film at some point. It will give you an interesting effect.

In late fall or early winter during the early evening, you will see a bright constellation, Orion, in the eastern sky. To early observers it resembled a hunter. What do you think it looks like? The three bright stars—Alnitak, Alnilam, and Mintaka—are easily seen and are often referred to as Orion's belt. The bright star Betelgeuse can be found at the hunter's shoulder. Rigel is near his knee.

What happens to Orion's position in the sky as the night passes? What happens as winter turns to spring? Can you see Orion in the summer?

The Constellation Orion

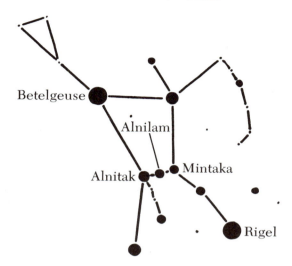

If you are interested, try to identify other constellations and follow their paths across the sky during the night and from season to season. What do you find?

MAPPING THE SUN'S PATH

To map the path of the sun along the celestial hemisphere, you will need a large, fine-mesh, dome-shaped strainer or a clear plastic dome. (You can probably find a strainer in your kitchen.) Place the inverted strainer or dome on a sheet of heavy cardboard. Mark the circular outline of the strainer's base with a pencil. Then make a heavy dot at the center of the circle. The dot represents your position at the center of the celestial hemisphere. Put the dome or strainer back in its original position and tape it to the cardboard.

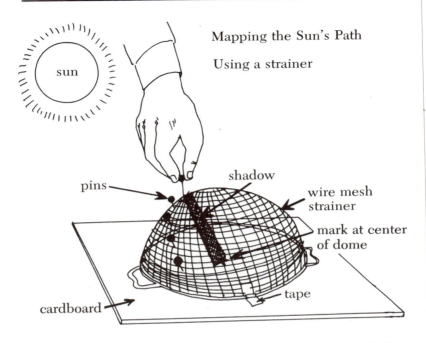

Mapping the Sun's Path

Using a strainer

sun

pins

shadow

wire mesh strainer

mark at center of dome

tape

cardboard

   Put the strainer outside on a level surface in full sunlight as soon after sunrise as possible. Place some weights on the cardboard to keep it in one position.

   If you use a kitchen strainer, you will need map pins with spherical heads. Put a pin in the strainer so that it casts a shadow on the center dot on the cardboard (see the drawing). The pin represents the position of the sun in the sky. Place pins in the same way every few minutes throughout the day. By sunset, the pins will form a pattern that reveals the sun's path across the sky.

   Leave each pin in the strainer after you have marked the sun's location. You may need small pieces of tape to hold the pins in place. At the end of the day, run a piece of colored yarn or string through the places where the pins were located. Then you will have preserved a record of the sun's

Using a clear dome

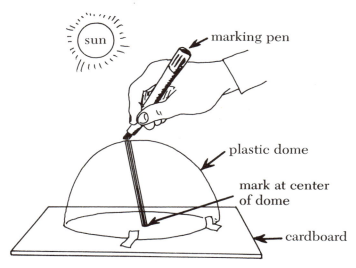

marking pen

plastic dome

mark at center
of dome

cardboard

path as it moved across the sky during the day.

If you use a plastic dome, place the tip of a marking pen on the dome so that the shadow of the tip falls on the dot at the center of the circle. Mark that point on the dome with the pen. Make marks like this on the dome every few minutes throughout the day. By sunset, the marks will form a pattern that reveals the sun's path across the sky.

Make similar records of the sun's path across the sky at different seasons of the year. Again, it would be good to record the solar path at the beginning of each season or around the twentieth of each month. Different-colored marking pens or yarn will enable you to see how the path changes.

What happens to the sun's path across the sky as the year goes on? How can you explain these changes?

WATCHING THE MOON

The moon doesn't always cast shadows, since it can often be seen in the daytime, but you can develop a good idea of the path it follows if you observe it frequently and record its position. Your record should include the time that you see it, its altitude, its position in the sky, and its direction of movement. You will notice also that the shape of the moon changes with time. A small drawing of the moon each time you see it will prove useful.

What do you notice about the moon's shape during the course of a week? A month? Does the moon always rise at the same time? In the same place? Are there times when you can't see the moon even when the weather is clear? Where is the moon in relation to the sun when the moon has the shapes shown in the drawing on the next page?

After you have watched the moon for several months, see if you can explain why the moon changes its shape and rising time from day to day.

A GLOBAL VIEW OF THE EARTH

Remove a globe from its support stand and put it outside in the sunshine. It can rest on a large empty can. Turn the globe so that the town you live in is at the very top. After all, that's the way the earth looks to you! If your globe doesn't come apart, you can tip the stand to get the globe in the proper position.

Turn the globe so that its North Pole points at the North Star. Use a small chunk of clay to fix a

Moon Shapes

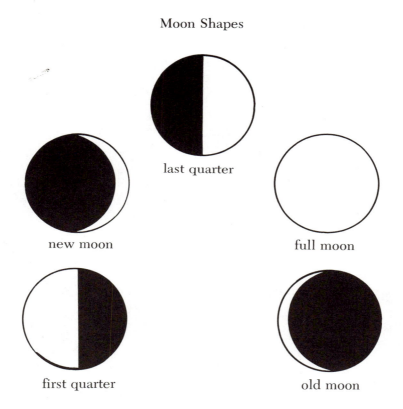

last quarter

new moon

full moon

first quarter

old moon

pin to the top of the globe. The pin represents you standing in your location on earth. Its shadow will point in the same direction as yours.

Now stand back and take a global view of the earth. Imagine that you are in a spaceship looking at earth from afar. Where is it dark on earth right now? Where is the sun rising? Setting? Is there any place on earth where the sun will not shine today? Are there places where it will not set? What time of day is it now in Hawaii? In New York? In New Delhi? In Hong Kong? In Oslo?

An object perpendicular to the earth's surface will cast no shadow when the sun is directly above it. Using a short piece of soda straw with a pin pushed through it for a handle, find a place on the globe where the sun is directly overhead. See if you can predict where the sun will be directly overhead one hour later. Test your prediction in an hour to see if you were right.

As the day progresses, what happens to the parts of the globe that are in darkness?

Let a ball represent the moon. Where is the moon relative to the globe when the moon appears as it does today? Where is it when it is a full moon? When it is a new moon?

What else can you learn by watching and experimenting with this global view of earth?

Repeat this experiment at different times of the year. What changes do you see?

HOW MANY STARS DO YOU SEE?

When you look up at the sky on a clear winter night, how many stars do you think you see?

To find out, cut a square 4 inches on a side from the center of a cardboard sheet. After some time, to allow your eyes to adjust to the dark, hold the sheet exactly one foot in front of one eye. Without moving your head, count all the stars that you can see through the 4-inch square. Move the sheet so that you see a different segment of the sky and count again. Make ten such samplings from a clear sky. Add up all your counts and divide by ten to get the average count. Your view of the sky through a square 4 inches on a side, when held one foot from your eye, covers $1/56$ of the celestial hemisphere's area. (Do you know why it is $1/56$ of the area?) Consequently, to make a good estimate of the total number of stars visible, you should multiply your average count by 56.

How many stars do you estimate are visible? Would the number change if you viewed the sky through a hazy atmosphere? Through a telescope?

Use an estimating technique to find the number of blades of grass in a lawn; to find the number of leaves on a tree; to find the total volume of rain that falls on your yard in a year.

8

BACKYARD PHYSICS

You don't need a physics laboratory to conduct experiments that help you understand the world you live in. In fact, you can carry on a number of investigations in your yard or park that would be difficult to do in a laboratory.

STAYING COOL

In Chapter 5 you may have built a hygrometer to measure humidity. You probably wondered why the wet-bulb thermometer had a lower temperature than the one with a dry bulb. To help you answer that question try these experiments.

Hold a thermometer in a breeze or swing it through still air to create air flow around the thermometer. Repeat the experiment, but this time put a little warm water on the bulb. How does the temperature change of the wet bulb compare with that of a dry bulb?

After a few minutes you will notice that the thermometer bulb is no longer wet. What happened to the water?

In a liquid, some of the molecules that are moving fastest escape from the liquid and become a gas. This process, called evaporation, causes the liquid to disappear slowly.

As temperature decreases so do the speeds of molecules. Since the slower molecules are the ones left behind in evaporation, a liquid tends to cool when it evaporates.

But why does the temperature difference between dry- and wet-bulb thermometers depend on humidity? The answer is related to the rate of evaporation in moist air. Water evaporates more slowly into air that contains lots of moisture than into air that is dry.

To see the effect that the rate of evaporation has on temperature, try this. Using a measuring cup, pour equal amounts of warm water into three identical aluminum pie pans. Submerge a thermometer in each pan and measure the water temperature in each. Keep evaporation close to zero in one pan by covering it with plastic wrap. Place a second pan in a protected spot out of the wind, but don't cover it. Put the third pan in a breezy place or in front of a fan. Record the temperature in the three pans at one-minute intervals for a few minutes. How do the temperatures compare? After a few hours, measure the volume of water that remains in each pan. How does the rate of evaporation affect the temperature of a liquid?

MELTING GLACIERS

To meet the water needs of the people during a drought, the officials of one country (Chile) had charcoal dust spread on glaciers high in the Andes Mountains. To see why they did this, place an ice cube in each of two identical containers. On one ice cube sprinkle some dark dirt or scrape some graphite from pencil lead. Place both containers in sunlight. In which container does the ice melt faster? How do you explain these results?

MEASURING SPEED

A fast-moving glacier may move 200 feet in one year. To measure speed we divide the distance traveled by the time it takes to go that distance. The speed of a glacier might be 200 feet a year. In more common units of speed, that translates to 0.0000043 miles per hour (mph)—a value too small to be understood by most people. The speed of light is so great that it is normally expressed as 186,000 miles per *second*, not 670,000,000 mph.

Police use radar to measure the speed of cars, but you can measure in another way the average speed of cars, cyclists, joggers, or walkers passing by your yard or playground. Place two markers 100 yards apart. As a car passes the first marker, a friend can signal you to start timing with a wristwatch second hand. When the car reaches the second marker, you can determine how much time has elapsed. (A stopwatch is helpful here, though not essential.)

The table will enable you to find speed based on the time to travel 100 yards.

**Table of speeds in mph based on
time to travel 100 yards.**

Time (seconds) to travel 100 yards	Speed (mph)
41	5
20	10
14	15
10	20
8	25
7	30
6	35
5	40
4.5	45
4	50
3.8	55

SWING TIME

The time it takes for a swing to move back and forth once is called the swing's *period*. Do you think the weight of the person sitting on the swing will affect the period? If you have a swing in your yard or park, you can easily find out. Measure the time it takes you to make ten complete swings after someone gives you a little push. Then let people of various weights sit on the same swing and repeat the experiment. (How can you find the time for one swing if you know how long it takes to make ten swings?)

Does weight affect a swing's period?

Does the length of the swing affect its period? If you can't change the length of your swing, use those in a park or playground that has several swings of quite different lengths.

What do you find?

SLIDING FRICTION

If you have a slide in your yard or playground, you can investigate friction. For example, how is the speed at which you descend the slide affected if you slide while seated on your sneakers? If you slide while seated on a piece of felt? On a chamois or flannel shirt? On a newspaper? On other materials?

Do heavier people, sitting on the same material, move down the slide faster than lighter people?

FALLING OBJECTS

Drop a heavy ball and a light one from the same height at the same time. Which ball falls faster? Or do they fall together?

Next, drop a ball and a sheet of paper. Which one reaches the ground first? It looks as though air somehow reduces the rate of the paper's fall. To test this idea, place a sheet of paper on a thick board or book that is bigger than the paper. Now the air cannot push directly against the paper. Drop the book with the paper on top. Does the paper fall differently than it did before?

Squeeze the paper into a tight ball. Predict what will happen if you drop the paper ball and a heavy ball from the same height at the same time.

Galileo is said to have dropped two balls, one ten times heavier than the other, from the Leaning Tower of Pisa to prove that objects fall at the same rate regardless of weight if air resistance is small. Galileo wanted to test his hypothesis in a vacuum, but he didn't know how to make one.

More than three hundred years after Galileo's death, astronauts dropped a feather and a hammer side by side on the airless surface of the moon. As expected, the objects reached the ground at the same time.

Maybe you have seen such a demonstration of objects falling in a vacuum at a science museum.

Galileo believed that an object would continue to fall at the same rate even if it was moving sideways. To find out if he was right, draw a target on a sidewalk or path. Ask a friend, riding a bike, to drop a stone, ball, or water balloon when the object is directly over the target. At the moment your friend releases a "projectile," you should drop another from the same height. Watch carefully and repeat the experiment several times. Do both objects reach the ground at the same time? Does the object moving sideways fall straight down onto the target, or does it continue to move along beside the bicycle as well as downward? Where should the object be dropped if it is to hit the target?

Here's an even simpler experiment. Drop a bouncy ball such as a lacrosse or tennis ball as you walk swiftly along a sidewalk or driveway. Have a friend drop a second ball from the same height. Do both balls hit the floor at the same time? Do you have to stop to catch the ball as it bounces up or does the ball move along with you? Try the experiment again, but this time stop immediately after you drop the ball. What happens to the ball?

One way to observe the path that a falling object follows if it is moving sideways is to watch water flowing from a garden hose pointed horizontally. What kind of path do the water drops follow?

A ROLLING OBJECT

What kind of path does the rim of a wheel make as it rolls along the ground? You'll be surprised when you actually map the path.

To find the path, tape a marking pen firmly to the rim of a tricycle wheel, a metal pail, or any round object that can be rolled along a sidewalk or path. Have someone hold a long piece of cardboard upright against the tip of the marking pen, sticking out from the wheel. The pen will map the rim's path on the cardboard as you slowly roll the wheel along the ground. What kind of path does the rim make?

FALLING DROPS

What happens when a raindrop hits the ground? To find out, let some water drops fall from different heights onto a piece of paper taped to a sidewalk or driveway. You can use a medicine dropper to make drops. Adding some food coloring to the water will make the splash patterns formed by the drops easier to see. As the drops fall through greater heights, does their splash pattern change?

How does the pattern change if the drops are moving sideways when they are released? Can you predict what will happen to the pattern as you increase the drop's sideways speed?

Are the splash patterns different if the drops fall onto different surfaces? You might like to try wood, concrete, soil, aluminum foil, and others.

Be sure to try wax paper. Wax repels water and should make a splash pattern that is quite different from that of a paper towel, which absorbs water. Can you guess what the splash pattern on wax paper will look like?

THE PUSH/PUSH-BACK LAW

It was Sir Isaac Newton who first gave the world a satisfactory explanation of motion. He said that when a force (a push or a pull) acts on an object, the object speeds up or slows down, depending on the direction of the force. He also said that if one body pushes on a second body, the second body automatically pushes back on the first with an equal force in the opposite direction.

To test these laws of motion you'll need a friend to help you. Both of you should be on roller or ice skates. While at rest and standing behind your friend, indicate that you are going to give him or her a push. Who moves when you apply the force? Or do you both move? Does the same thing happen when your friend does the pushing? What happens if the person you push is much heavier or lighter than you? To push something very much heavier than you, push against a post or building. In this way you will be pushing against the earth. Why?

Do your experiments confirm Newton's laws?

PUSHING A BASEBALL

You have seen the path followed by a falling object that is also moving sideways. All you need do is watch the path of a water stream emerging from a garden hose. Use the same garden hose stream to predict the angle at which you should throw a baseball to make it go farthest. Obviously, an angle of 90 degrees above the horizontal will give the ball a distance of zero. It will simply go straight up and then come back down. You'll want to try this angle with the garden hose only if it is a hot day.

Once you have made a prediction, try throwing a baseball at different angles. In each trial try to throw the ball with the same force. Approximately what angle gives the ball maximum distance?

Suppose you are an outfielder and want to throw a ball to home plate in the least amount of time possible. Should you throw it at the angle that gives maximum range? Should you throw it horizontally and let it bounce several times? Or should you throw it at some other angle?

To test for minimum time, have a friend use a stopwatch to see which kind of throw gets the ball there fastest.

BUOYANCY IN POOLS, PAILS, PONDS, AND OCEANS

Can you float in fresh water? How about salt water? Even if you can't float, you certainly fall much more slowly in water than in air. Consequently, there must be some kind of force pushing upward on you in water. To test this idea, hang a heavy object (a stone or a piece of metal) from a string. Then lower the object into water. What seems to happen to the stone's weight? To find out how much the weight changes, hang the stone from a spring balance. Note the weight of the stone. Then lower the stone into a pail of water. How much weight does it lose in water? What kind of objects have no weight in water?

To see the presence of such a force in another way, find a balloon or a ball that floats. Hold it as far under water as you can reach. What happens when you release the balloon or ball?

Backyard, rooftop, pond, and woods, the world you live in is full of intriguing life and questions. Using the equipment and techniques you've learned about in this book, you can go on exploring the science that you find all around you.

APPENDIX

Science Supply Companies

Carolina Biological Supply Co.
2700 York Road
Burlington, NC 27215

Delta Education
P.O. Box M
Nashua, NH 03061

Edmund Scientific
101 East Gloucester Pike
Barrington, NJ 08007

Nasco Science
901 Janesville Road
Fort Atkinson, WI 53538

Schoolmasters Science
P.O. Box 1941
Ann Arbor, MI 48106

Ward's Natural Science
P.O. Box 1712
Rochester, NY 14603

INDEX

ABOUT THE AUTHORS

Robert Gardner is chairman of the science department at Salisbury School, Salisbury, Connecticut. He has taught at a number of National Science Foundation teacher institutes, including one in Ajmer, India, and was a staff member of the elementary science study of the Education Development Center. Mr. Gardner is the author of a number of books for young people, including *Kitchen Chemistry*, *The Whale Watchers' Guide*, and *Science around the House*.

David Webster teaches elementary science at two schools in Massachusetts. He was a staff member of the elementary science study of the Education Development Center. Mr. Webster has written sixteen science books, including *Track Watching*, *How to Do a Science Project*, and *Spider Watching*. He lives in Lincoln, Massachusetts, and spends summers on Bailey Island in Maine.